The Bee and the Acorn

Published by Assouline Publishing
3 Park Avenue, 27th Floor
New York, New York 10016
assouline.com

ISBN: 9781614285083
Printed in China
First edition

ILLUSTRATIONS BY Emily Isabella
(B.F.A., fibers, 2008)

AUTHOR PHOTOGRAPH BY Adam Kuehl
(M.F.A., photography, 2014, B.F.A., photography, 2005)

DESIGNED BY Rosa Triolo
(M.F.A., graphic design, 2013)

PACKAGED BY Design Press Books, a division of SCAD

The Bee and the Acorn

A MEMOIR BY
Paula Susan Wallace

ASSOULINE

For all the dreamers who came to SCAD and found
their people, and for the dreamers yet to come.

Contents

A Letter to the Reader

The work of writing, like all artistic creation, is part technique, part inspiration, all magic. Something happens when words brush up against one another, cascading down the page through the riffling of sentences and paragraphs. The words do something; they turn into a story.

My life portrait has been guided, sustained, enlivened by vignettes that string together like Sargent's pearls. That's what each of these stories is, a single pearl, added to another, and another, until there's a whole string of them.

In the elementary school classrooms where I began my career as an educator, I captured the attention of my young students with stories, mesmerizing their wild, beautiful minds with tales from the Secret Garden, Wonderland, Oz, Narnia, Camazotz. And when we created the Savannah College of Art and Design nearly forty years ago, stories were how we kept our sanity. In 1978, it was just the four cofounders—my parents, May and Paul Poetter; my first husband, Richard; and there was me, still very much the ingénue at twenty-nine.

But even before then, before SCAD's doors opened and the first classes began, we were joined by others, our vibrant new colleagues who came to Savannah from around the world. We'd gather in one another's homes and share stories about where we'd lived and worked before coming to Savannah, what we missed, what we loved about this fascinating place, draped in moss and shadow and cut through with the purest Atlantic light, a place we now called home. I remember long nights, on balconies and bluffs, from the marsh to the river, rocking my daughter to sleep while my new colleagues and I swapped stories. We swatted away the gnats, quelled our laughter so as not to wake the baby, and shared our deepest hopes and fondest dreams. I was so happy to be part of a circle, to have others around.

If gifted, credentialed professionals were willing to move across the country to join our happy little band, I thought, then maybe this was more than a fantasy. Maybe it was real.

After a decade, then two, in Savannah, when it became clear our little school was going to thrive, stories became something more, a way for us to create tradition, to mark how far we'd come. We initiated new members of the college community with stories about the hurricane, about the first-ever day of class, about how all of us once licked admission mailers every Friday until our tongues didn't work right, about how we built a college library from books left uncollected at the post office, misdirected to addressees unknown. About the time the academic dean had to go diving into a dumpster with a student, to rescue the student's final project.

I've never forgotten the aroma. Or the ecstatic "Eureka."

These stories—and a thousand more—became the stuff of legend, the currency of the college, and as the college got older, moving into its third decade and into a new millennium, these stories became history.

"Remember the time when..." I'd hear myself saying.

"This reminds me of that day we..."

"We did something just like this back in—was it 1997?"

The only difference was, by the year 2000, so few people remembered. Many of the veterans of our first decades had retired, moved on. Some had passed away. Suddenly, before my eyes, the college was home to a new sea of faces, people who didn't necessarily know the who, the where, the why of how SCAD came to be.

"I wasn't here then," they'd shake their heads.

"What?!" they'd exclaim in astonishment.

"I had no idea," became a repeated refrain.

That's when the desire to write this book was born, I think. I usually wave questions away when people want to know what it was like back then, when it all began, how we got from there to here. After all, one pearl leads to another when you're stringing a necklace that rests close to your heart. How could I possibly fit all these memories into one book?

Though I've never been a fan of long, lumbering tales thick with words, I wish I could exalt every person, every student and friend and colleague who has walked this road with me, through tears and triumph, laughter and loss. But alas, I cannot. The girth of that tome would be more suitable for pressing wildflowers and clover.

The Bee and the Acorn does not masquerade as a definitive, unabridged, complete history book. Facts can be found here, yes, but memory is what lives in these pages. If there is more sunlight than shadow, it's because that's how I choose to remember, and because some stories are others' to tell. If I have a vision for this book, a hope, it's that this will be a story about joy, a book of celebration filled with gratitude for this life, for the friends and family and colleagues with whom I've shared it.

Recently, one parent of a student described SCAD as his son's "dream school," a place of "high-tech environments, warm people, good vibes." This, he said, was our "brand." And maybe it is, but there's something else, too: magic. There's always been magic in this place. And there is magic still.

Prologue

From far down the hall, through a labyrinth of corridors beneath the vast arena and beyond curtain after curtain of black muslin, came the first familiar notes of the orchestra. A march as everlasting as the rotation of the Earth, the gentle flourish of strings, the wave of sound as blithe as clouds on a halcyon day. No song can stir the butterflies in me like Elgar's "Pomp and Circumstance," that definitive call to commencement, the ending of one season, the beginning of something new, when time folds, collapses, unravels, gets knotted up in memory, and the heart leaps and soars into the past and future all at once.

"It's starting!" cried someone at the front of the room. "Line up! Line up!"

We were in the greenroom deep down in the belly of the Savannah Civic Center, the largest venue in town, and our small prep room was packed tight with buzzing Bees in regalia, students and staff and special guests in swishing robes of wool, everybody flitting about nervously with the morning's electric hum. I stood alongside our commencement speaker, John Lasseter, Pixar's chief creative officer, chatting with the students who would be marching in with us.

"We're starting!" someone said.

"Are we starting?" I asked.

"How do I look?" John asked.

"The picture of wisdom and grace," I said. "Break a leg!"

"You too."

A man named Danny called us to queue. He is one of the most patient men I've ever known, with silver hair over a boyish, puckish face, a man who can command a room with grace and good humor. He watched us as we darted about, and he called us again.

"It's time, ladies and gentlemen," he said, without a hint of pique. He used to be a teacher. You could tell. I looked around and realized: So many of us found our way to the Savannah College of Art and Design by first and always being teachers.

Our train snaked through the room as best it could, while Jody, my assistant, buzzed up and down the line, adjusting everyone's hoods and caps, tucking and blousing and pinning, half of us looking over notes and pages. Like nearly all sane human beings, I get anxious before speaking in public, and I found myself reading my speech over and over while Jody fussed with my hood.

"Your cap's all wonky," she said.

"We're moving!" Danny said. "We're about to move, ladies and gentlemen!"

The line tittered and rustled. We straightened up, got quiet.

I looked around at this roomful of educators and marveled at how many of them felt like family, men and women who have worked alongside me to build this moment together.

Jody came back, whisked the master script out of my hands, and gave me a clean copy.

"This one has all your changes," she said.

I jumped out of the line, sneaked behind a curtain, and found Stephanie, our valedictorian, a brilliant young jewelry designer from New Jersey, clutching her speech notes for one last quick rehearsal. How many times had I found valedictorians just like this, nervously mouthing their remarks while everyone lined up?

"I'm a little nervous," she said. "But I think I'm ready."

"Just remember," I said. "It's your moment."

"I might pass out."

"I'll catch you."

"Do you get nervous before a speech?" she asked.

"Oh, yes. Heart palpitations. I almost passed out once. The first commencement."

"How many people were there?"

"About twenty-five," I said.

"How many people are here today, do you think?"

I pulled back the curtain and looked at the monitor mounted near the door, the camera panning. "About ten thousand."

"That seems like a lot."

"Just have fun," I said. "And smile. And remember—everybody out there is family."

"Okay, thanks."

We hugged.

"Go!" Danny said.

We went.

My life had led me to this processional moment, to this train of regalia, marching through a sea of smiling faces toward an impossibly large stage, where the tears in my eyes turned the lights into diamonds.

We marched brightly through the valley of robes and up toward the stage, and I looked up, where images of the past academic year flashed across the screens, pictures of recent history, now gone. I have nothing against the past, but the past has had its chance. Forward—that's my favorite place to look. You can paint whatever you want there. Maybe that's why I love stretching toward the future in a line, where everybody's looking ahead and nobody can see my shining eyes.

I looked to the distant stage, where John and I and deans and students would soon be standing, and as we marched, I felt the years pass across my mind's eye and through my heart. What I saw, coming into focus, was the image of myself sitting at a narrow cafeteria table where, in many ways, all this began.

Chapter One

Impossibilities

In 1977, the world was ready for something new. All around us, dreamers were dreaming up new ideas: *Star Wars*, The Clash, Apple. I was nearing thirty fast and wanted to do something new, too. I'd been teaching elementary school in Atlanta for seven years and loved it, but I wondered if I could do more.

"What's on your mind, Paula?" said the man across the table. Here was no mere man, but the one, the only, the immortal Charlie Pepe, my supervisor, the principal of Sarah Smith Elementary in Atlanta, Georgia. He was larger than life, always in a tie and always laughing, sitting across the table with a mouthful of food, nodding, eyeballing my plate once his was empty.

"Do you mind?" he would ask, forking a piece of chicken off my tray.

"Please," I'd say.

But that day, he wasn't looking at my food. He was looking at me.

"Pardon?" I said.

"You appear to be lost in thought, young lady."

Charlie was very much of the old school, the sort of administrator who once roamed the halls of so many public schools across the nation, as full of opinions as lunch, a ring of keys and a head full of stories at the ready. He was a native of Brooklyn and a graduate of Tufts but seemed as Southern as you might expect an Atlanta principal to be, with a jowly smile and a playful twinkle in his eyes. For me, he was part boss, part mentor. He could talk the hind leg off a mule, as my mother would say, but he knew how to listen, too.

"What's on your mind?" he said that day in the cafeteria, as I sat alone, making notes in a notebook I'd kept hidden from everyone. He glanced at it. He wanted to know what I was working on.

I knew if I told him, he'd laugh.

But I had to tell him.

"I'm thinking about starting a new school," I said.

"Ha!" he said, bringing his hands together in a thunderclap. He smiled.

I'd been thinking where my career might go next. I was young but already had several years' experience in education, mostly in elementary schools. Likewise, my husband, Richard Rowan, was an educator, having served as an administrator at secondary schools and colleges around Atlanta. I'd been back in my hometown for nearly a decade and enjoyed my work with students immensely, but some unnamed ambition had come alive in me, and I found myself wanting more. Could I do it? Start a new school?

I'd been wondering when to bring it up to Charlie. I knew his reaction would speak volumes. If he believed in somebody, he let them know it. He was not full of false praise. But when should I bring it up? When is the best time to announce a crazy idea to your mentor, so as to seem as uncrazy as possible? At the end of the school day? On the playground? No, the only time to make crazy seem good, at least to Charlie, was at lunch. Food always put him in the most sanguine mood.

"What kind of school?" he asked.

"An art school," I said. "For children. For students like mine."

In ten years of teaching, I'd learned a lot about what was right and wrong in education. I'd done my student teaching in the Greenville Public Schools during forced integration and busing, when, in a flash, half of my students were gone, replaced by new students. I'd been teaching for only a few weeks when it happened and didn't know enough to be anxious. When you're twenty-one years old, everything's an adventure. Later, I taught for a year at Ebenezer Elementary in Travelers Rest, South Carolina, and then in the early seventies I moved back home and settled into my life in public education. I don't know how it happened, but I became a sort of itinerant teacher in the Atlanta Public Schools, getting placed in challenging classrooms that needed solutions. Every year, it seemed, I'd get a new call.

"Will you go to Garden Hills?" someone from the central office would ask. Sometimes it was E. Rivers, Cascade, Warren T. Jackson, Sarah Smith, among other schools.

"Sure," I'd say. "Why not?"

This response became a sort of trademark.

Because why not? Every yes was a new door. I felt like Alice in Lewis Carroll's adventure, whose story I'd started reading to my students wherever I went. Here was a story about flexibility, about being open to the world. I wanted my students to see that sometimes you have to grow tall and big to get through a new door, and sometimes you have to do the unexpected thing and grow small.

What I learned in those early years of teaching was this: Old institutions don't change much or ever. Too many rules, too much to risk. If you want to do something new, you can't do it at an old place, at least not if anybody's looking. And in my classroom, nobody was looking.

"Challenge the students," Charlie would always tell me. "Surprise them. Do something new. Go for it."

And surprise them I did—with stories.

"Today, we're going on a journey," I'd say. "But I won't say where."

"Awww," they'd say in unison.

All day, I'd hold their attention with everything from popcorn to Popsicles and this promise of an adventure. And then, when they least expected it, while all the other students in the school building were facedown in textbooks, I'd line up my students and march them out to the playground.

"It's not even recess!" they would say, in awe of the wide world like it was a new thing, and we'd go searching for colors, shapes, and ideas related to our lesson.

Sometimes I took them on journeys with books, ending the day with a chapter from *A Wrinkle in Time*, leaving them on the edge of their seats, only to close the book as the bell rang, their eyes wide with wonder.

I wanted every student to feel like Alice, every classroom to be its own Wonderland. In graduate school at Georgia State University, I'd studied gifted education, which helped me understand the power and value of arts education. I came to see if you wanted to engage advanced students—really, all students—you had to engage their imaginations. In arts education, everything was more intense: more joy, more passion, more work, more effort, more freedom. I was a born rule follower, a typical oldest child—meeting deadlines, staying in my assigned grooves—which helped keep me organized and focused, two things every teacher needs to be. And yet, teaching art and music and creative writing gave me liberties I hadn't known were there. By teaching young students how to create new stories and songs and art, I'd begun to create my own new story.

...

Suddenly, to my surprise, I became the rogue teacher, taking students into undiscovered territory, at least into no territory I'd ever studied in any education course. I had the students making filmstrips, writing literary journals, transforming the classroom into a Calderesque circus, performing original musicals, orating from a stage that my father, Paul, helped me build right there in the classroom.

"We do have permission to build this?" Dad asked. "I mean, the principal knows?"

"Yes, of course."

Honestly, I didn't remember. I do remember thinking that it's easier to ask for forgiveness than permission. When Charlie eventually saw it, he loved it. He trusted me. While other teachers were lucky to get permission to take their students to the zoo, we were loading up those children and driving to the *Treasures of Tutankhamun* exhibition seven hours away in New Orleans. On the way, my young students and I discussed archaeology, painting, and sculpture, what museums are and do, and why it's important to study art history.

I'd taught my students to expect more, and now I was expecting more, too, asking the question I'd taught my students to ask: What will happen next? I couldn't get away with all this experimentation for long, all these field trips and construction projects, this dragging of pianos and instruments into the classroom. I wanted to build a place where every teacher could teach like this.

"It's your fault," I told Charlie. "You're the one who put this idea in my brain, letting me take my students on so many adventures."

"I thought you loved your class," he said.

"I do," I said. "And I want to create a whole school just like it."

I wasn't the first person in my family to bring up the possibility of creating a new school, but those conversations had centered on starting a new college of some kind, not an arts academy for elementary or secondary students. I'd considered it. But no, my interest was primary school. I loved teaching children, who looked up to me, literally, because they were quite short. It was nice being the tallest one in the room for once.

"It could be a magnet school," I said to Charlie. "It wouldn't be freewheeling. We'd have a mission. We'd have concrete goals. We'd show results."

With my master's degree in curriculum and instruction, I knew it could work. I'd find ways to measure what we were doing.

"What about funding?" he asked.

He just didn't see it happening, not with the bureaucracy of public school administration, all the permissions and approvals, the politics of it.

"Why not make it a college?" he asked.

"An art college?"

"Isn't your husband in college administration?"

"Yes, but—"

"Listen," he said. "Starting a new elementary school in this town would be a nightmare. But anybody can start a college."

This time, it was I who laughed.

...

A college for the arts?

Really? I don't know, maybe Charlie was pulling my leg, just trying to keep me from leaving, but all day, all week, I couldn't stop thinking about it, as though saying the idea out loud had released more than words into the air.

My heart felt freer, too. It felt realer.

One summer, during a break from studying at Furman, I learned a lesson from my father about believing impossible things. He had gotten me a job at the Continental Insurance Company in a high-rise near the old Loew's where *Gone with the Wind* had premiered. I was a bookkeeper—a pretty standard role for a woman in the sixties—and spent all day entering premiums into a ledger. It was exhausting work that deadened the mind and soul. The floor where I worked was clouded all day in a haze of cigarette smoke, and I had only thirty minutes for lunch.

"How's the new job?" Dad asked, after a week or so.

"It's fine," I said, trying to not sound ungrateful.

"You hate it," he said.

"I do."

"What you have is a job," he said. "What you want is a profession."

For a father to say this to a young woman back then was no small matter, not in the South. He hadn't even finished college, though his skill with numbers had given him solid footing in the U.S. Bureau of Labor Statistics. My mother, a teacher and supervisor of other teachers, had earned two degrees in education, one at the University of Southern Mississippi, which she earned in the fifties with two children in tow, and a second at Emory, when we were older.

"Your mother did the impossible," he said to me, after one of these long hot days at Continental, explaining that if I didn't find a profession like she did, then I'd be like so many others, locked away in a smoke-filled haze with my nose in somebody else's ledger.

A decade later, I looked at my young students and wondered: What would they do when they got to college? Where would they go? Would there exist a university like this classroom, where the hands readily made whatever the head dreamed and the heart loved?

...

"Are you still considering that wild idea?" Charlie said one spring day, several months after our first conversation. By then, my notebook was chock-full of ideas for what this new college could look like.

"Absolutely," I said. "Why?"

"Call my wife," he said. He wrote her number down. She ran the art department at Agnes Scott, the small women's college near Atlanta. "See what Marie has to say."

I thanked him, and that night, called Marie Pepe.

She was kind, but didn't have much positive counsel. She was even more candid than Charlie and did not try to hide her opinion behind the niceties of conversation with a new acquaintance.

"I wouldn't do it," she said. "I mean, what sort of experience do you have starting a new college, much less an art college?"

"None."

"Where will you get the money?"

"I don't know."

"How will you get students?"

"I'm not sure."

She wished me well, said she'd say a prayer for us, but the phone call shook me up a little. I wondered if Charlie had put her up to it. After all, he stood to lose me from his faculty roster. Maybe he was trying to spook me into staying? No, no. His heart was too big for skullduggery. Maybe he was just trying to steel my resolve. Maybe he thought Marie's tough questions would wake me up to what I needed to do. The economy was not getting better, and soon it was the spring of 1978 and about time to start signing teaching contracts for the new school year.

"I don't have your contract yet," Charlie said in the office one day at school. "You're not still thinking about that art college thing, are you?"

I knew signing the contract was the smart thing to do. How crazy was it to give up the only job I'd ever loved?

In a fearful moment, in my classroom, while all my precious students were gone for the day, I signed my contract and promptly locked it in the desk. Could I go through this door? Was this normal? Is this what artists felt like? I was feeling more and more creative and unbound every day, with my students, in my classroom, and with this new idea of a new college. Something was different about me. I could feel it.

My husband would resign his position at the university, he said. He wanted this as much as I did.

Everything was about to change.

...

One Sunday after church, I lingered over lunch with my parents at their new home out on Pace Road, their dream home.

"I have some news," I said.

"Is this about that school you've been talking about?" my mother, May, said.

We'd already started searching for a location, a building in Atlanta, although it was starting to seem like Atlanta already had too many colleges and universities—at least enough institutions to dwarf a tiny new art school. I called every art department and art school in North America and asked for a course catalog. I wanted this new school to be distinct, to be just like what I was doing in my classrooms—a marriage of measurable results and perfect surprise.

"The school?" I said. "Yes. The school."

My father, I knew, would support anything I did, but my mother was harder to please. She was an educator, too, and she knew what it took to make a school thrive. She was a language arts supervisor for a large number of the school system's English teachers, and she'd already authored two language arts textbooks for Houghton Mifflin, a project I'd helped her with in graduate school. She'd tucked away those monthly royalty checks for their retirement, and now they'd built this home in the country.

"How will you pay for all this?" Mom said. "A new school needs money."

Sometimes my mother got you on your heels. But this was her way. She had a keen mind and could drill down to the heart of any conversation in a heartbeat. She did not play games.

"We'll do what we need to do," I said. "We're going to sell everything. Our car, the furniture, all of it."

"Where will this new school be?" Dad asked.

"Atlanta already has too many schools," I said.

We'd already imagined all the possibilities—Charleston, St. Petersburg, St. Augustine—places we'd visited, all within a few hours of home. But none felt right. Except one.

"What do you think of Savannah?" I asked.

"There's nothing in Savannah," Dad said. "It's so small."

"And old," Mom said.

"And beautiful," I said. "I think students will love Savannah."

Things were quiet for a while, just the sounds of forks on plates.

"We're not sure you ought to do this," Mom said.

"But—"

Here was the woman who'd shown me how to do impossible things, and now she was barring the door I wanted to push through.

"You have no money," she said.

My heart sank.

"I know," I said.

"Which is why we want to help."

"Help?" I said.

I could hear emotion in her voice.

They'd give us what was left of their retirement savings, she said, so we could go off to this little place called Savannah and see about building a dream.

"Besides, maybe we can sell this and get something smaller?" she said to Dad.

"It's too big anyway," he said.

"You will absolutely not sell this house," I said.

"Our children are the dream, honey," she said, taking my hand. "Not the house."

"We're proud of you," Dad said.

"There's something else," I said.

"What?"

How should I say? I didn't know. So I just said it.

"I'm pregnant."

"I knew it!" Mom said.

Dad broke into a huge grin.

"I hope my grandchild likes to play Crazy Eights," he said.

We hugged and laughed and talked. Girl? Boy? Names? We'd been trying for a while and I'd tried to forget we were trying. And then, wow. A baby. A school. A dream.

Suddenly, nothing seemed impossible.

...

The next day, I found myself back in my classroom at Sarah Smith, trying to imagine a life somewhere else, in a building I hadn't seen, a building we hadn't bought, far away in Savannah. Was it really happening?

"Knock knock," came a voice from the doorway.

"Charlie."

"So, about that contract?" he said. "I've got everybody's but yours."

"Should I really be starting a school now?" I asked. "I mean, with the baby?"

"Why not?" he said. "Isn't that what you always say?"

I opened my desk, pulled out the signed contract.

"Give that here," he said. He snatched it from my hands and in a single, joyful motion, tore it up.

"Charlie!"

"I always knew you'd go on to do something great," he said, smiling.

Nature had made up my mind for me. New school or not, I would not be teaching elementary school in the fall of 1978. The runway was clear for everything and anything. The coming of the new baby didn't crowd out the dream of a new college—anything but. The new baby was a sign: We could make something new.

The standard dictum about professional women is that we all have to make the crossroads decision: baby or career? Many women have to make that choice for a thousand different reasons, but in my case, the baby made the career possible. The baby freed me from the contract I knew I'd have to sign. Without that beautiful baby, this dream may have never happened.

"So, I guess you'll be the president of this new school?" Charlie said.

"Oh, no," I said. "Not me, no thank you. I'll handle curriculum."

"So a dean then?"

"I don't care what they call me."

"I'm going to miss you," he said, extending a hand. "And so will your students."

I pushed his hand aside and hugged him as hard as I could, my eyes filling with tears. I was leaving behind so much that I loved, about to push through a door to a whole new Wonderland.

Chapter Two

Guardians

"I don't think I can do this," I said to the real estate broker. "Go without me."

It was early December, and I was very much in the condition of Mary of Nazareth. Every day I felt ten pounds heavier. The baby in my belly seemed to like it when I was on my feet: I'd bounce a little; the baby would bounce a little. I kept moving, which is what brought me here, to these many steps in this citadel, where I wasn't sure I could go any higher.

They called it the Armory. It was silent, cold, damp, dusty, gargantuan. Many years later, students would nickname it "Hogwarts." But in 1978, the building had no heat, no air. It was a thirty-six-thousand-square-foot fortress of a thing, with peeling paint, every surface coated in a greasy, lurid dust. Many windows had been boarded. In one window, in lieu of boards, hung a Schlitz beer sign.

"Go for the Gusto," the sign read.

The Gusto, it appeared, had gone too.

And yet, I loved it, the history of it, the castle-like aspect of its façade. The grime could be cleaned. The Gusto could return. But there was one thing I worried about.

"I think maybe it's way too big," I said to our broker.

"Yes," the broker said. "Huge."

For a second, I thought she might be talking about me.

The building served as headquarters for the Savannah Volunteer Guards. Could we make an art school in a ponderous old building like this? Could we transform a hall designed for military drill into a library? Could these weapon rooms become studios? I loved the paradox of it, the surprise. That's what I wanted for our new school, surprise. The unexpected. Something nobody would see coming. I adjusted my little navy dress with the Peter Pan collar and grabbed the banister.

"I'm coming up!" I said to the air, my breath rising with me.

...

As a native Atlantan, I'd grown up hearing stories about old Savannah. It was provincial, small, they said, belonged more to the past than the present. Since the Civil War, the story went, all the action had moved to Atlanta, as had many of the people. Those who knew the city still spoke fondly of her, with words like *little, sleepy, quiet, old*. Lovely, yes, but not necessarily the sort of place you start a new college of art.

I'd visited on a long weekend in 1974, and something about it stayed with me. I've always been enchanted by objects with history, even when they're a little battered. Old vanities, old silver, the Old Masters. My first home in Atlanta was a 1930s carriage house, frightening off potential renters with its chipped paint and eerily naked windows. I loved it, painted it, sewed my own curtains, transformed it. That's what I saw in Savannah—the promise to make something new, with history. Maybe it was foolish, but then, instinct has often triumphed over logic in my life.

"Why Savannah?" family friends asked, when we told them our moving plans.

"It's historic," I said. "The architecture's elegant, everywhere you look. And the beach is twenty minutes away."

"Have you been downtown?" they said. "It looks apocalyptic."

And yet: The light was luminous, I explained. As were the squares. Students would love painting and drawing and studying in the squares. The weather's great all year. The city will be the classroom, I told them.

"If they don't get mugged."

"They won't get mugged."

"How do you know?"

I wasn't sure. Faith, maybe.

By the time we actually moved, faith was about all we had left.

To finance the new college, we sold nearly every stick of furniture, whole wardrobes, books, lamps, the beloved black and yellow Volkswagen Beetle, even a new home we'd just finished building, after the first home we'd built burned to the ground owing to a cigarette carelessly tossed by a neighborhood boy.

All we had left were a few books, a few boxes of clothes and kitchenware, and not enough furniture to host a yard sale.

We still hadn't enough money to fund a new nonprofit, much less a new institution of higher learning, until my parents gifted their entire retirement account to our little dream.

"Take it," Dad said.

"God has his hand on this," Mom said.

So that was it, we were officially poor and homeless, and my parents had no retirement.

In Savannah, we found a small two-bedroom condo on a quiet island, far away from downtown. The city's core was vacant—block after vacant block, so many of the streets and avenues lined with crumbling façades, homes that looked worn and fragile and tired, as if a good gust of wind would leave them in pieces. And yet, there remained saintly old churches and the occasional distressed goddess palace that took your breath away, especially around Forsyth Park.

In the evenings, the sun would dapple through the airy quilt of trees guarding the city from above, the light dancing across the lacework of iron on the balconies, a fairy-tale light. I loved that light. It's what brought us here. But the locals joked about downtown, made excuses for why they wouldn't move back.

"It's full of ghosts," one friend said, the week before our move.

The Armory had no ghosts that I could see, but had something even stranger roaming the wide hallways.

...

They called themselves many names: the old generals, the officers, the captains. These were the few lingering officers of the Savannah Volunteer Guards, whose fathers and forebears had fought in every American war since before the nation even had a standing army.

Their story goes all the way back to 1751, when the colonies had to raise their own defense, a luxury not provided by the Crown. The Savannah Volunteer Guards, consisting of local merchants, farmers, and professionals, sent men to fight in the War for Independence, the War of 1812, all the way up to both world wars. But by 1978, the Armory was merely a social club, no longer a storehouse for uniforms and firearms. Instead, it became a meeting place, a dance hall, a place for long and lavish dinners.

By the time we found ourselves walking its grand corridors with our real estate broker, there were only a few of the old generals left in the building, puttering around, their old regalia and flags and guidons and uniforms on display, grown brittle with age. Many were already in their eighties and nineties. Some had fought in the Spanish-American War. One claimed to have fought against Ulysses S. Grant, which would've made him at least one hundred twenty-five years old, but you could tell: He believed it.

"We're about too old to keep it up," one said.

They wanted to know why we wanted to buy it.

"We're starting a new college," I said.

"Ha!" he wheezed. He was genuinely surprised.

"I think it's great," another one of the officers said. "Savannah's a fine place to start a college. We started the University of Georgia right here."

He was right. One of America's first public universities had been chartered not far from where we stood, back in 1785—when Savannah was the state capital. Richard and I had been looking for potential properties all fall—old schoolhouses, abandoned hospitals, a morgue, empty factory warehouses, vacant downtown department stores, a deserted power station. At the time, none of us could know that eventually all those properties would become part of what we were going to build here.

"There's an old casket factory," the broker said.

"Casket factory?" I said.

Savannah was getting more curious by the hour.

Artists were going to love the city, I knew that. But were they going to love the Armory? The architect, William Preston, from Boston—another stranger from out of town, like us—had studied at the Académie des Beaux-Arts in Paris, and he'd brought advanced techniques to the project, using massive iron I-beams in the structure. Until that point, iron was for railroads, a burly, beefy material that belonged on the ground, not up in the rafters, but Preston had learned innovative methods for bending and manipulating iron. I liked that, and I liked that he'd learned these techniques at an art school. Even more, I liked that his ideas meant something: the egg-and-dart motifs in the plasterwork suggestive of the social function of the space, Bacchus looking down from every corner of the dining room, the bas-relief heads of the lion god Apademak on the front mantelpiece signifying conquest, the inverted fleur-de-lis, a jest at the French. There was wit and intellect and a playfulness here, the profile of Tomochichi in plaster, chief of the Yamacraw who lived on these bluffs. I reached up, ran my fingers over the face, the mouth, the eyes, wiping dust away, climbing up, eye to eye with the bas-relief.

Here was a man who'd welcomed the first Europeans.

Was he welcoming us? Would he let us live in his building?

It was too big, too old, and too expensive. But it was beautiful.

"There's a problem," the broker said, a few days after we made our offer.

Had we been ambushed, outbid by someone who didn't like the idea of these strangers moving to town to do a new thing?

Savannahians had shown us great warmth and friendship. This was, after all, the Hostess City of the South, a town known for charming its guests, wooing them with parties and balls and never-ending dinners and bottomless highballs filled with artillery punch. They had once charmed Generals Washington and Lee, who had visited for pleasure, and even General Sherman, who visited on business with a book of matches. Surely this was a community that would welcome students from around the world.

"Did they accept our bid?" I asked.

"No," she said. "They have to vote first."

Apparently, there were nearly two hundred members, each belonging to an old Savannah family, who'd be deciding our fate.

Everything moved slowly here. I was accustomed to the electric whir of Atlanta, but here, the days were unhurried, indolent. Banks closed in the middle of the day. Every day. Savannah, it seemed, was still powered by steam.

"The problem is that some of the members are not going to give you their votes."

"But why?" I said. "Is it us? Is it because they just don't like us?"

"No," she said. "Because they're dead."

It was around that time that I went into labor.

...

My daughter, Marisa, was born on December 31, 1978. She weighed nearly ten pounds. If she'd been any bigger, we could've shared dresses.

"Where are we on the Armory?" I asked between feedings.

"We've got a battle on our hands," President Rowan said.

"I thought they liked us," I said.

He explained: A local group had made a move on the building once they'd learned we were trying to buy it.

"For what?"

"An inn," he said.

I was worried that maybe we had made enemies with someone. The last thing Savannah needed, back then, was another bed-and-breakfast.

The local group consisted of two or three investors who were using their influence to snatch the building away, despite our good-faith offer. We might as well have been the British in 1779 or Sherman in 1864.

"I don't know," President Rowan said. "Maybe they don't like us because we're from up north."

"We're from Atlanta," I said.

"Exactly."

I called my parents for advice.

"Don't you worry," Mom said. "Once your college is successful and well known, they'll love what you're doing. They'll all want to jump on the boat then. You just wait and see."

The officers finally decided to make a vote on our bid, and ballots were mailed out to every member. We waited. And waited. The mail was slow. Everything was slow. It started to feel like it really wasn't going to happen.

And then, aid came from the most unexpected place. One of the organization's younger members—at age sixty, he was practically a babe in arms—saw that the missions of the Savannah Volunteer Guards and the new college were similar in many ways, that both organizations existed to serve their communities. This young member of the Guards wanted to help us, and he got in his car and visited the homes of all the unreturned ballots. He would reason with them, explain how a new college might give the building the life it needed. He even volunteered to go to the library, to the microfilm, to confirm that indeed many of the unreturned ballots had not been returned because those officers had marched ahead to the great battlefield in the sky. They made the adjustments to their roster and balloting, and, when all the ballots had finally been counted, they brought us the news.

"You got it!" the broker said.

The building was ours.

...

After uncorking a bottle of prosecco, we went home to bed, relieved and happy, but I couldn't close my eyes. The elation of our winning the building was wearing off quickly. I stared at the ceiling.

Was this foolish? What were we doing here, all our worldly possessions poured into an empty building that smelled of soot and unpolished leather? I'd bought plenty of papier-mâché and crayons for my students over the years, but never an armory.

I heard a sound. It was little Marisa, nearly three months old now, as she cooed in her dreaming. I went to her bassinet.

"We're going to build a life here," I whispered. "We're going to make a college."

Now that we had a building, we needed a name. We'd tossed around a few ideas, but nothing stuck. I wanted something that caught in the air when you said it, a name that sounded new and curious and durable.

The Art College of Georgia.

The Southern School of the Arts.

The New College of the Beaux Arts.

Nothing worked.

I thought about putting Savannah in the name somewhere. I wanted to show the city that we wanted this to be our home, that we wanted Savannah to be a part of it all, that we wanted our little school to be a part of this grand old city's new history.

"The Savannah Volunteer Guards Armory was a good name," I said to my mother, when they were down, visiting, to see the new building their retirement had bought. "We could do something like that. Like, the Savannah Art College."

"How about the Savannah College of Art and Design?" Mom said.

It seemed a little long, but then I saw it, saw the letters. I could see it in front of me, out there in the air, on a sign, a shirt, a banner, in front of an armory. SCAD.

Yes.

SCAD.

Chapter Three

Bohemians

We stood on Bull Street, the long, thin avenue running through the heart of the city like a spine, flecked with light and leaves, canopied squares along it at intervals, verdant vertebrae holding the city together. Our building lived on one of these squares, Madison Square, although the guards, now gone forever, had called it Jasper Square, after Sergeant Jasper, the man whose statue stood in the center of the square. He'd fought the British and died in the Siege of Savannah, the second-bloodiest battle of the American Revolution.

Now that the building was empty, it looked even bigger. I worried we'd oversold ourselves, had spent a quarter of a million dollars on a building in a ghost town.

"I love it," Dad said.

"The students will, too," Mom said. "When they get here."

But would they ever come?

"That building's haunted," a passerby said, clearly mistaking us for tourists. Soot and mold clothed the brick like an old garment, turning it a foul color, and the wide, lovely windows of the first floor were boarded for some long-forgotten hurricane. The first floor alone was a testament to failed entrepreneurship, the old soldiers, in a strategic retreat, having let out most of the ground floor for a greasy spoon, a secondhand shop, a nightclub.

"Well, Paul," my mother said. "I never thought we'd use our retirement money to purchase a nightclub."

"I always did like to dance with you," Dad said.

They were so giving, so willing to give of themselves to their children, their communities. And Savannah wasn't even their community. They still lived in their dream home out on Pace Road outside Atlanta, but the dream was quickly becoming something else. They'd been broken into twice. The first time, the burglars had taken jewelry, silver, what objects of value they could carry. The second time, they'd taken everything that would fit in my father's car, and then they'd taken the car, too.

"It was a smart heist," Dad said. "One had to respect the efficiency of it."

"Oh, let's not dwell on it," Mom said.

"That's why we like coming down here to Savannah so much," Dad said. "We have to give the criminals their space."

"I may start leaving sandwiches out for them."

As I listened to them jest like this, back and forth, suddenly they seemed younger, and—despite their homeowner woes—seemed filled with a lightness that I didn't necessarily feel, not right then. I had a new baby and a new burden, and this building needed serious work.

"Where do we start?" Mom said.

"The grease traps," I said.

We started with the space in the corner, the old diner. The place was rancid, rank, the detritus of a thousand breakfasts caked to the ceiling, the walls, the floor.

"What y'all cooking?" a man off the street said, after we'd thrown the doors open.

"Art," I said, wiping my face with a forearm, the world's tiniest chimney sweep.

"Must be putting a bed-and-breakfast in here," he said.

"It's going to be a college," I said, explaining that I was the academic dean.

"A who?"

"This will be our gallery," I said, "and there's our president right over there, with the hammer."

President Rowan introduced himself, and they got to talking about our plans while I returned to my scrubbing. I usually felt more comfortable behind the scenes; my father was much the same way—quieter, more to himself. I found him in the old night-club, scrubbing the walls.

At my childhood home in Atlanta, my father loved to build, build, build, including little rock gardens, which he'd seen in the Far East during his time in the war. He was always making some-thing, digging out basements, installing new floors, constructing new backyard walls from stones he'd found in a river. Having his help here was key. But this was no rock garden.

He'd brought in a little radio and found a country music station.

"I figured a nightclub needs music," he said.

I made my way up the stairs, through cobwebs and over holes in the floor, looking for the balcony. From there, I found the street, the square, the city all around. Much was ruined, wrecked, boarded, gloriously beautiful and derelict. Across the street, the Scottish Rite building seemed an ornate slice of wedding cake off a Greek temple, but hollow, vacant, gray with age. What the city needed was young people, and I couldn't shake the worry that they might not come.

"We don't need a bunch of punks downtown," I had overheard one local say to another at a cocktail party, when news of our art school got out. "We've already got punks."

"They'll be bohemians," said another. "And hippies."

"Sounds communist."

I just smiled. Would they have purple hair, as was suggested to me by one wary business owner? Or pink? Or strange pierc-ings and shredded clothing, and did it really matter? It had never occurred to me to care about the color of anybody's hair or the flavor of anyone's ideologies. We were building a college. They could be Whigs and Tories and Union sympathizers with nose rings and sandwich boards and Bibles and I wouldn't care, as long as they wanted to learn to make something beautiful, and make a living doing it.

...

From the balcony, I could hear my parents working down below. They were as curious to me as Chief Tomochichi in the other room, these people I'd thought I'd known so well, who were surprising me anew every day. They'd given their life savings to the college, and had begun coming down every weekend to work. They should've been sitting on the front porch of their dream home outside Atlanta, but here they were, sleeves rolled up.

There was magic in their marriage, that was sure. On paper, it was conventional—a veteran who'd served as a statistician for the government, a mother who'd been a schoolteacher, both Southern, hardworking, the very definition of conventional. But in other ways, they were anything but. I couldn't put my finger on it. Whatever their secret was, it was going to take some of that same magic, I felt, to make SCAD fly.

They met during World War II, when she was volunteering with a church group that organized farewell parties for soldiers going off to war. My father spotted her right away, followed her around all night, asking her again and again to tell him her name. It sounds funny now, to think of my father chasing after anything except a receipt.

My mother just shook her head, refusing.

"Just tell me your name," he said.

"Who knows if I'll ever see you again?" she asked.

"I bet I can guess your name," he said, "and if it's right you have to tell me."

"Fine," she said, looking for some route of egress. She was too sensible to fall for a young man about to find himself in alien lands, full of glory and adventure and war. But he was too earnest. "Okay, mister. What's my name?"

"Layla Lane," he said with confidence. According to her, she audibly gasped. Layla Lane? What kind of a name was that? Her name was May. Willie May Lewis.

"Layla Lane?" she said. "How did you know?"

They wouldn't see one another again for nearly two years, but that hadn't stopped him from wooing this new friend with words, writing her a trunkful of letters, which my mother kept locked safely away, each one addressed to Miss Layla Lane.

...

Many years ago, I found a postcard that my father had written, not to my mother, but to his parents. He'd been stationed in Hawaii after Pearl Harbor, and the postcard depicts a field of pineapples, stark and green and stretching to the horizon.

"Nothing goes to waste here," he wrote. "It's all either pineapple or sugarcane or coconut." There was as much wonder as tender sadness in his words, a longing. "There's coconuts everywhere—as much coconut on Hawaii as there is homesickness in me."

His fascination with the industriousness and endless ingenuity of Hawaiians, especially when it came to those pineapples, was no accident. He'd come of age in the Great Depression and knew how to stretch a dollar and reuse a sheet of aluminum foil. Jars, cans, old socks found new lives with Dad. A Gerber jar that had held strained peas for my little sister soon held penny nails in the basement.

"Why are you throwing away my favorite green socks?" he'd ask.

"Because they're no longer green," Mom would say. "And they're no longer socks."

When she forced some of his old undershirts into retirement, he merely reassigned them to duty as oil rags for the garage. Nothing wasted, everything used.

"Everything gets tossed," I explained to him in the short-order diner.

"These countertops look solid," he said.

"They're ratty and old!"

"A little paint, a little love."

I looked at my mother for help.

"Sorry," she said. "We think he was born this way."

We assigned a room in the back of the Armory for Dad to place all his "projects." Our plan was to let him fill the room, and then we'd empty it after he'd gone back to Atlanta.

"He's hoarding ketchup bottles," I said to Mom, in a whisper.

We laughed, but also, we had no money. The idea of saving ancient ketchup bottles wasn't that far-fetched. We'd already saved this building, hadn't we?

A man like that, I thought, should be in charge of our budget.

In my youth, I remember him coming home from the office with a case of typewriter ribbon. "What is all that?" Mom said.

"For the typewriter."

"That's for a Smith Corona," she said. "We've got an Underwood."

He kept those Smith Corona ribbons for years, stuffed high on a shelf in the basement, evidence to us of a slight, if innocent, derangement. To him, it was crazy *not* to save them. And when they moved from that house a decade later, he sold the box. For a profit.

"See?" I remember him saying to all of us, cash in hand.

A man who could find a use for a box of old ribbons could come in handy around a fledgling school that needed to rub its pennies together. He was a singular man, equal parts bookish and brawny. After high school, he'd even been awarded a football scholarship to Auburn, but the war intervened. After the war, Dad took a few college classes and apprenticed with a controller, staying in the role of analyst and researcher for nearly thirty years until his retirement from the U.S. Bureau of Labor Statistics. He was awarded the Distinguished Service Award, the highest award given to a civil servant by the United States government.

The man knew how to account for money.

Yes, we could use someone like that.

We could also use someone with a spirit like his, full of light and love and literature. He loved to recite "The Charge of the Light Brigade," shouting, "Half a league onward!" when going to battle with a resistant fence post or hauling heavy flagstones for a new patio. All through my youth, I'd catch him and my mother reciting memorized verses across the yard, the house, in a playful dialogue. For many years, I thought it was perfectly normal for one's parents to recite Tennyson at the dinner table.

He didn't allow himself many luxuries, but he loved to sit quietly on the front porch on summer afternoons and listen to his beloved baseball games on the radio. Those are my happiest memories of him, when I was next to him on the porch swing on Montrose Avenue in Atlanta, him listening to the Atlanta Crackers while I sat with a book in my hands, feet curled under me, leaning my whole weight against him as I nodded off.

...

If Dad was our Gibraltar, then Mom was our ocean, moving, rising, covering the world. She was the youngest daughter of eight children, liable to be trampled underfoot if she lingered anywhere for too long. She grew up on a farm in Collins, Mississippi, a land of white clapboard houses and pastures about one hundred miles north of the Gulf.

With so many older children handling the chores—the milking, feeding, cleaning, sewing—my mother's only task was to stay outside, away from all the work, and she did, carrying a book with her to sit under the wide, fat magnolia just beyond the kitchen garden, where she leaned against the tree and read and read, all day, every day, until, it seemed, she'd read every book in the Collins Public Library.

Those books swept her away to distant lands, in heart and mind. In the late 1930s, when most of her friends were being married off to farms around Smith County, my mother dreamed of getting an education at the Mississippi State Teachers College in Hattiesburg, later called the University of Southern Mississippi.

She first enrolled at Hinds Community College, near Jackson, but the Second World War had a way of changing everyone's plans, and soon she found herself in Atlanta, where she met my father and became Miss Layla Lane for the duration of the war. After they'd married and had two young daughters, she still hadn't given up that dream of finishing college. And in the fifties, when my little sister, Pam, and I were still very young, she made it happen.

In summers, we left Atlanta for rural Mississippi, leaving Dad to man the fort alone for many weeks while Mom began earning credits toward her B.S. in education. Our grandmother Olive, Aunt Bess, and Uncle Bud were there on the farm to look after Pam and me while our mother made the nearly hour-long drive every day down U.S. Highway 49 to attend lectures and seminars.

During those long, languid days, I found myself wandering out into the yard with a book to sit under that tree, under the very same shade where my mother sat, to embark on the many adventures our books had in store.

I can remember *Little Pictures of Japan*, a large blue book of illustrated haiku, an elegant 1925 edition with gilded lettering, gold spine, delicately illustrated endpapers. I imagined myself in exotic locales, lifting tiny cups at tea ceremonies and bowing to Japanese princesses under the shade of cherry blossom trees. I had perhaps a dozen or so books just like this one, each about a different destination, a distant land, each volume a portal.

I'd fall asleep with these books across my lap, dreaming about the strange place my mother had gone to—a university, she called it. I pictured her there, passing through the shadows of brick and stone and ivy that I'd seen in photographs, living this life of the mind, and I'd wake up late in the afternoon, my dress clinging to my legs from sweat, and hear the sound of Mom's car crackling up through the gravel of the driveway.

"I'm home!" she'd say.

Heaven knows she must have been tired from a full day of classes and the wearying drive back to the farm, but she smiled brighter than the evening sun on those days, letting us bury our heads in her pleats and follow her into the kitchen to help Olive with dinner.

"You ought to read this," she said, one evening after we'd cleared the table, setting the *Anthology of Children's Literature* down next to me on the bed. I was seven or eight at the time, and this massive volume was a compilation intended for teachers-in-training, not for young children. This must have been my mother's way of prodding me to greater things, to something beyond the short form of the haiku and Aesop.

"What's it like at the college?" I asked one night. "Where do you get all these books?"

And she told us once again about this university, its buildings, lecture halls, library.

"A library the size of a department store," she said. "You must see it sometime. Rows and rows of books, stacked to the ceiling."

It sounded dreamy, like a place where one could spend a life.

...

Twenty years later, my mother had not stopped telling people about the glories of higher education; only now, it was our college.

"SCAD is the best thing to happen in education in a long, long time," she'd tell anybody who'd listen. I noted her use of the present tense, even though we had no students yet.

"You must work in admission," these Savannahians would say.

"Oh no," she'd say. "They don't even have an admission office yet."

"They should hire you."

I began to give it serious thought.

"What do you think?" I asked President Rowan one day, as we were mapping out a recruiting calendar for the coming months. There was much work to do. "Mom would be great at this," I said. "Just look at how she talks to people about the college."

I tried imagining what it would be like, my parents—these two very traditional Southern Baptists–turned–Southern Methodists, conservative, buttoned-down, archetypally Greatest Generation—being the first two hires of America's newest art college. They were the antithesis of every art cliché abounding at the time, anything but boho.

But were they, really?

Here was a man who had no college degree and who'd risen to the highest levels of civil service, who'd saved enough money to build his own home, which he'd planned to do with his own hands, and a woman who'd earned two college degrees when other homemakers barely had permission to walk beyond their front yards. She'd risen to the highest levels of her profession, too, had started clubs, founded churches, written textbooks for literally millions of English students around the country, all while being a mother. And here they were, already having invested their retirement into a crazy startup in a town they barely knew.

They were the true bohemians, the original Savannah hipsters, their lives evidence that boho wasn't to be found in the color and style of your hair, but in the heart.

"Let's ask them," President Rowan said, one weekend when they were in town to work on the building.

It was spring in Savannah now, and they had made a dozen trips back and forth to help us gut the building and get it ready for faculty interviews and admission tours. They were tired of driving, and we were tired of waiting for them to come back every weekend.

"Mom, Dad," I said.

We sat in the ballroom, the great, wide-open space on the second floor, eating lunch at one of our worktables, the same old kitchen table where we had first discussed this idea a year before.

"There's something I've been wanting to ask you," I said. "We thought if you were already coming down so much…"

"Yes!" Mom said. "Yes, we'd like to move."

"We would?" Dad said. "No, it's not a bad idea, I guess. Moving should be easy. The burglars have taken most of what we own."

"You could use the money from the sale of the house," Mom said.

"She's right," Dad said. "If you want it."

"A couple of young kids like you will likely need a job, since you gave away your retirement," I said.

"Wait," Dad said. "I thought we were retired."

"Oh, hush," Mom said. "Retirement was boring."

"Okay, I'll work here," Dad said. "But only if I can be the football coach."

After hugs and a brief moment of celebration, we were back at work, and I found myself on the third floor, looking for cleaning supplies on a small interior balcony that overlooked the ballroom where Mom and Dad were scrubbing. The Guards had used it for drills and dances, and their commanders had often stood on these balconies, observing. I imagined military and USO dances right here on the eve of war, just like the kind where my parents had met, a soldier and his sweetheart, Miss Layla Lane, and their enduring bohemian love.

Down below, I heard Dad's radio, the tinny AM sounds of country music filling the cavernous space, and heard a laugh. I peeked over the edge and saw him take Mom by the hand and lead her across the floor to dance.

"Get to work, you two," I said, smiling, and they pretended not to hear.

Chapter Four

Hurricanes

The Armory became our second home. We'd found a little residence twenty minutes away, but for all intents and purposes, we lived in the brick colossus on Madison Square, lugging in most of our remaining furniture—sofas, chairs, clocks, lamps—to make it homey. When we needed more furniture, we acquired it in strange places, such as the mysterious warehouse off the highway between Savannah and Macon called Surplus Property, a giant world of ever-changing *objets trouvés*—bookcases, diving helmets, jumpsuits, parachutes, and other items from decommissioned military bases. We acquired a number of metal desks there and painted them bright colors. From the very beginning, this was our way, to revive, repurpose, renew.

We spent months cleaning, scrubbing, and polishing to my mother's exacting standards. I'd spent my childhood doing the same on Montrose Avenue, where every Saturday was Chore Day, Pam and I on our hands and knees and tiptoes dusting every square inch until we squinted from the glare. My mother had a special gift for putting children to work, compelling us to polish even the wooden dowels on the backs of our Windsor dining chairs, pressing into our hands endless cans of Hagerty Vernax Furniture Polish.

"Mom, why are we doing this?" I would ask. "There's no dust."

"That's because you dust it every Saturday," she'd say.

Twenty years later, we applied the same polish to the woodwork of the grand staircase in the Armory, where every day was Chore Day.

"Why are we doing this again?" my mother asked, as we applied the third coat of polish.

"Revenge," I said, laughing, as we worked our way up the stairs.

And then, in August 1979, six months into our habitation of the Armory, it seemed as if everything we'd cleaned and polished and prepared was about to be destroyed. We were on our hands and knees again, and instead of smelling furniture polish, we smelled the sharp odor of ozone and the coming of a terrible storm. All around us trees cracked and fell, battering the walls, cracking windows, snapping power lines.

"This isn't good," I said.

"They say it's going to get worse," President Rowan said.

"Hurricane David," said the man on the radio, which my father operated in the corner, searching for the latest news. This storm, the one whose overtures we heard entering the city just now, had already killed thousands in the Dominican Republic.

"Winds of one hundred fifty, maybe two hundred miles per hour," the radio announced.

I touched the walls of the building. Would they hold? We'd given the building a name: Preston Hall, after its designer. The walls he'd designed were three feet thick, I reminded myself.

"This was an armory, remember," Dad said. "They had munitions here. Gunpowder. They thought the British might actually come back. This was their Alamo."

"Yeah, I remember how that story ended," I said.

Preston Hall seemed in no condition for a test. It was still very much a construction site, with buckets and scaffolding and tarpaulins and the smell of paint and new carpet.

We were on the second floor, all of us, the whole family, grandmother and grandfather and daughter and son-in-law and Baby Marisa. Like everyone else, we'd been told to evacuate our little home on one of the islands, surrounded by marsh and tidewater. Most sensible residents had retreated far inland, to Macon and Atlanta and elsewhere, but we couldn't leave. Everything that mattered to us was right here. We couldn't retreat from Savannah now, at the first sign of trouble. We were here to stay. If the city got washed away, we had nowhere to go but with it.

"This is the strongest building in Savannah," Dad said, more a prayer than a declaration.

...

"Is she sleeping?" Mom asked, candlelight dancing across the walls, giving the room an ancient glow.

With one hand I rocked the bassinet we'd brought from home, with my other hand I held a pencil I'd been using to edit our first catalog by candlelight. The catalog had long since been completed and mailed to high schools across the country, and I was already beginning to think about the second catalog, reworking sentences, reconsidering word choices. The college was discovering who it was, and words were a way to do that. How we talked about SCAD was the reality of SCAD. Every word mattered. I've never been able to put down the editing pencil, even when something's finished, when it's gone to press. More than once, colleagues have had to pry reports and catalogs from my hands.

Besides, as the weather turned angrier, the mood more anxious, I was grateful to have something to keep my hands busy. I scanned the catalog for typos I'd missed, but those were hard to find by the unsettled flickering of tapered candles. Outside, Savannah was black and hot and loud. David was tearing the city apart.

"How many deposits do we have?" I asked Mom.

"Thirty," she said.

Thirty students. In the past few months, we'd recruited thirty students, mostly by mailing posters, welcoming curiosity seekers into our amateur construction zone, visiting high schools in Georgia, Florida, and South Carolina, and attending college fairs in the Southeast. Was that enough to make a college? I didn't know. It wasn't in the book. There was no book about how to start an institution of higher learning.

"God's hand is on this work," Mom said behind me. She would say it many times over the coming days and years.

Why hadn't we opened a college in Atlanta, or somewhere else where the weather couldn't kill you? It seemed foolish. Suddenly, we heard a loud screech, a terrifying, shrill sound.

"What's that?" I said.

We ran to the windows and saw it: a large sign, ripped off the façade of the pharmacy across the street, hurled by the wind onto the bricks of Bull Street, rolling wildly, hitting parked cars, until it was gone.

A burst of shattering glass.

"Were those our windows?"

We had sixty windows, and most of them were brand new.

President Rowan ran toward the sound, flashlight in hand, my father not far behind.

"Be careful," Mom said.

I watched them leave and turned to the baby in my arms, now stirring at the sudden crash. Marisa's eyes were open again, looking, moving, full of questions, as were mine. Class was set to start in mere weeks. Would the students come? Would our college be here when they arrived? Was it okay to have more windows than students? I was the dean of academics, but I was also in charge of human resources and exhibitions and events and publications. I was also executive chef, resident *pâtissière*, lead interior designer, dean of curriculum and instruction, and chair of every academic department, because we had no chairs—not yet.

I never really stopped to consider how unprepared I was, on paper, to help create a new institution of higher education. I probably couldn't have gotten hired at another arts university. I held a B.S. in elementary education and an M.Ed. and Ed.S. in curriculum and instruction. No gallery experience, no human resources experience, no anything experience but classroom teaching, really.

"What's your background?" parents would ask upon visiting Preston Hall with their students, curious about applying for admission. Sometimes they were prospective new faculty members who had been invited to campus to interview.

"Elementary education," I would say.

"So you have a Ph.D. in arts education?" they would say.

"I taught."

"Oh, so you were an elementary school teacher," they would say.

And they would look at me funny, sort of. If they only knew what I knew, that anyone who ever taught elementary school is more than a teacher. When you're standing there in kitten heels and a pencil skirt in front of a roomful of eager young people, you're also the chief grammarian, marshal of storytelling, events coordinator, calisthenics coach, arbitrator of disputes, playground referee, designated trip leader, captain of high fives and hugs, cheerleader, songleader, line leader, EMT. You do it all, and you do much of it alone.

But I could not do this alone.

...

Long before the hurricane threatened our building and our lives, I'd picked up the phone and called Teresa Norton, a friend from my childhood who'd gone on to study and teach painting in New York.

"I need help," I said.

I told her all about what we were doing, our college.

"You should come down here and teach," I said.

"Okay," she said. "What do you offer?"

"I don't know."

Silence.

"What do you mean?"

We stayed on the phone for a good three hours, mapping out what we would teach, what majors, ideal course sequences. It was heady, dizzying, fun. We already knew our college would distinguish itself by openly acknowledging what no other arts institution seemed to acknowledge at the time: Artists and designers need to earn a living.

In 1979, the reigning consensus of art and design education suggested that the words "creative" and "profession" shouldn't be in the same sentence. True artists, it was said, should not care about money, food, appearance, or the next job, and anybody who did was a sellout, a charlatan, or a bourgeois phony. This disdaining ideology infected arts education, which meant that colleges and universities willfully ignored what art and design students did after they left the institution.

I began reaching out to all the young artists I knew, and I asked them: Where did you go, and what are you doing now? Many of them had moved to New York and San Francisco, some even to London and Paris. They had all wanted to be the Next Big Thing—the next Warhol, to live the celebrity life.

In the meantime, waiting on the dream to come true, they'd engaged in all sorts of interesting work. Some had opened their own architectural photography businesses, others were illustrating children's books, many were working at museums, galleries, schools, and newspapers, interning, apprenticing. Some had been doing it so long that they were considering the possibility that the thing they were doing might be the dream they'd had all along.

"What do you wish you could have studied?" I asked.

"How to start a business," one said, and others said the same. They said they'd liked to have studied marketing, networking, and how to balance passion, career, and a budget.

"I wish somebody had explained how much public speaking I'd have to do," one young advertising art director said. "All I do is talk. All I do is pitch. And I write. I spend most of my day trying to get clients to believe in ideas. I had to teach myself how to do that."

I shared all this with Teresa.

We mapped it all out: We would teach students how to be accomplished painters, photographers, and interior designers, and we would also teach them how to market their work, how to speak, write, pitch. We would teach them to conduct research, win competitions, plot demographics, anticipate needs, and create ingenious products and services. We would offer literature, too, and history. All the liberal arts.

We chose eight majors: ceramics, graphic design, historic preservation, interior design, painting, photography, printmaking, and textile design.

I showed the first draft of the catalog to everyone.

"What do you think?" I asked. "No more starving artists."

"That should be our motto," President Rowan said.

We wouldn't ignore the realities of what students did after graduation. We would teach and learn together. And when the students graduated, we wouldn't lose touch. We would know right where they were. They would be working.

...

In those months leading up to the storm, while I continued to refine the curriculum and President Rowan set about getting to know community leaders, my mother spent her days scouring high schools around the South and up and down the East Coast for talented new students. In many ways, my mother was the ideal candidate for this role. For one, she didn't look like other recruiters, who back then were nearly all young and male, the standard uniform being khakis, a blazer, and a repp tie. And then came Willie May Poetter, this archetypal Southern lady who might arrive at a college fair in gloves and a hat, looking more like the spry grandmother of a prospective student than the recruiter.

She had manners, and she had pluck. Once, at a college fair in Florida, my mother introduced herself to the organizer. "Oh, yes, the Savannah College of Art and Design," he said. "The Harvard of art schools!"

"Really? That's what they call us?" she said. "Well, how nice for Harvard."

Her secret weapon in admission was her lifetime of experience in the classroom, allowing her to speak the language of guidance counselors and art teachers. She knew how to assuage the fears of parents on the fence, how to ask the right questions to lead students to discover the answers for themselves.

If I saw it happen once, I saw it happen thirty times during that first year. We would have an open house, and I'd see her by the door with a family and the wide-eyed student, and she'd be chatting with them like they had all been friends for years. As, indeed, she felt they had been. She would ask questions about what the student hoped to get out of an academic experience, and pretty soon, the student would open up, and Mom would start nodding, and then the student's parents would start nodding too.

"Yes, it will be wonderful," she'd be saying. "You will love it here. We have to have you. What would SCAD be without this bright talent!"

And the student would begin nodding too.

Before long, while the rest of us were just learning the names of the prospective students and their families, my mother would have them signing up for a parking decal.

"For when you get here in the fall," she would say.

And they would leave the event, smiling, believing in themselves, still nodding.

"You're good at this," one new faculty member said. "You must work in admission."

"Oh, sweetheart," she said. "At SCAD, everybody works in admission."

...

By late July 1979, we had hired seven faculty members and two or three support staff, and I had played a key role in most of those hires. I was twenty-nine years old and had never hired anybody to do anything besides mow a lawn. All of us were surprising one another. I was most definitely surprised when I received this note from my father:

> Dear Dean Rowan,
>
> Please explain the three long-distance calls made from your office on Monday and Tuesday of last week.
>
> Thank you,
> SCAD Accounts

I wasn't sure what to make of the note. This was my father, famed pincher of pennies and cincher of belts.

"You have to see this note," I said to President Rowan, who read the slip of paper.

"Oh, good," he said. "I thought I was the only one who got those."

...

Weeks before we had ever heard the name Hurricane David, fewer than forty students had committed to SCAD, and we had even lost some who had gotten cold feet. Savannah was too far away, they said, or the college was untested, or the student had friends somewhere else.

"We're losing enrollment and we haven't even held our first class," Mom announced one night at dinner.

We had to do something. We had only six weeks until classes started.

"Can we start early?" I asked.

"What?" she said. "You tell me. You're the dean."

I thought about all the field trips I'd taken my students on in Atlanta. Why couldn't we do that? Two weeks later, we were on a plane with two dozen new students and three new faculty members, on our way to San Francisco for what would become our first off-campus academic study trip. I chose this destination, in part, because *Treasures of Tutankhamun*, which had been making its way around the world for several years, was in San Francisco that summer. I had already taken my Sarah Smith Elementary School students to see this exhibition a few years before and knew our first group of SCAD students would love it too.

"Nobody does it like this," I remember overhearing one faculty member say to another at baggage claim. He was more seasoned, more skeptical. He had concerns that we'd organized this trip out of the blue, in the middle of the summer, before we'd even offered a single class.

"At least the college is paying for it," a fellow traveling faculty member said.

I had to smile. That's exactly what I wanted SCAD to be—the sort of place that did things nobody else did. The trip was a success, the students had a blast, as did the faculty members, and the nascent enrollment was reenergized. The week before the storm, enrollment had reached thirty students.

"How many do we need to break even?" I asked.

"Sixty," President Rowan said. "Maybe seventy."

"What will happen if we don't get seventy?" I said.

We all looked at one another, and turned to my mother.

"Faith," she said.

...

And the storm came, and the winds howled, and we held hands there in the dark of Preston Hall, our citadel, amid the roaring of the hurricane. Windows cracked, exploded, crashed.

Marisa stirred again, started crying.

I picked her up, tried to rock her, soothe her.

"We need more students," I said to my mother.

"More will come."

All night, and for the next three nights, we huddled, miserable, hot, suffocating, watching for looters, hail, tornadoes. We had left behind good jobs, careers, salaries, homes, communities, and people we loved, and now we had none of that. Everything had changed. I had changed. I'd done more than I ever thought I could. I'd built a curriculum, built a faculty.

This terrifying storm, I decided, could not hurt us.

Three weeks later, the sky was blue as a childhood memory, and the power was back on, the Armory lighted with electricity and sunshine and our smiling, eager faces. The clouds were gone, the doubt was gone, and faculty and students came pouring into Preston Hall for the first day of class, while we stood at the door and welcomed everyone.

They had come. All of them had come, and more.

We had seventy-one students.

Chapter Five

Books

In those early years, I worked in a constant state of wonder, wide-eyed and grateful for the people with whom I worked, for the students who continued to walk through the front door. This place and its people were a marvel.

"So, there's something we need," I said to the other three founders one day in the winter of 1980, during one of our many brainstorming sessions around the kitchen table.

"We need a lot," Mom said.

"We need a library," I said.

"How much will that cost?" Dad said.

"Not much," I said. "Like, a hundred thousand dollars?"

"Oh, that's all?" President Rowan said.

I explained that our first accreditation site visit would be happening soon, and we'd need to have something that looked like a library. So far, what we had was a closet with a handful of used art history textbooks. A college needs a library; we all agreed on that. But where? What would we do when prospective students and their families asked to see the library? Take them to the closet?

"You're the dean, you'll figure something out," Mom said, as I drove her to the airport for another admission fair somewhere in the Lower 48.

I watched her bound toward the ticketing desk, full of spirit and cheek and beauty, a curious combination of talents. I am fortunate to have spent a life surrounded by such curious women—grandmothers, aunts, teachers, colleagues, friends—who gave me clues about what a woman could be.

One thing they all shared is that they never mentioned any contradiction between feminism and femininity. It was not a part of their playbook. They were strong women, it always seemed to me. They were strong people.

My grandmother Olive was pragmatic and capable, unintentionally chic in her fuss-free wardrobe of cotton mid-calf dresses that draped over her slender frame. Olive's day began before the sun rose. Like a gifted dancer, she moved with a silent swiftness, when, whispering through the predawn hours, she fed the animals, tended to chores in the barn, baked biscuits in a skillet, their delicate scent gently rousing Pam and me from heavy sleep when we stayed with her in the summers.

Olive ran the estate, tending a bountiful vegetable garden with beans, peas, corn, okra, tomatoes, cantaloupes, watermelons. On the back porch were the well and wringer. In the yard, she boiled linens in a cast-iron cauldron and wrung them out before hanging them on the line. Olive could do it all.

During the day she wore a tight, center-parted bun at the nape of her neck for optimal efficiency, free of fuss and midday touch-ups. At night she would let it down, weaving the locks into a cascading braid for sleep. As a little girl, I loved to watch the ritual of it, gazing, fascinated, as she brushed out the knots from the day's work, plucking out a strand of hay, tying the robin's-egg-blue ribbon at the neck of her nightgown before she went to sleep. It was a fascinating transformation: my grandmother, a woman who ran a farm, who did it all, transitioning from work to rest.

Sometimes, our little art school felt like a family farm, and like my grandmother, I worked from before sunrise until long after sunset, and when I slept, I slept hard, and when I dreamed, I dreamed of libraries.

"Can you help us build a library?" I asked a young man named Steven Myers, a friend of Teresa's, who'd been teaching art history at Hunter College and wanted to move down South.

He thought it was a trick, something in the interview to trip him up. Then he paused, and the truth settled across his face. "Wait, you're serious?"

Over the next year, Steven and I sent letters to public and university libraries across the country. We shared our story, our mission, our need for books, any books, any and every book they had that was a duplicate or about to get tossed. And we waited.

And we waited.

Nothing.

And then, something.

"We have some books, if you're interested," the nice man on the phone said.

"Absolutely," I said.

Steven stood by my side, nodding eagerly. It was the State University of New York at Fredonia or Binghamton, I don't remember.

"Let me see what we have here—" he said, looking through his papers, over notes, whispering to this or that assistant librarian. We waited. "How does ten thousand books sound?"

Had he just said *ten thousand*?

I must've had a terrible expression, because Steven thought all was lost.

"What is it?" he said.

Where was my voice? My voice was gone. Something was caught in my throat. It felt like I'd tried to swallow a volume of the *Encyclopedia Britannica*.

"Yes, yes, thank you," I managed to squeeze out.

"A lot of them are law books," the man said.

"Yes, we'll take them."

"You're an art school, right?"

"We'll take them."

I thanked him, over and over, and we discussed the details, and I hung up.

"We did it!" I said.

"Yes!" Steven said.

My mother came in.

I hugged her, told her the news. We had our library.

"A law library!" Steven said.

The law books we put in storage.

"We could sell those," Dad said.

Maybe. They were beautiful. We could use them, somehow, I knew. Later.

In the weeks that followed, we got more and more calls, including one from the state librarian of West Virginia, who had been gathering art and design books from a public library that no longer had space for them.

"I want them to go to a good home," he said. "You just have to come get them."

I soon became the Pied Piper of Lost and Unwanted Books, traveling the country with a valise and a list of books our faculty members said our students needed.

On the road, I felt less like Olive and more like my father's mother, Gert, the free spirit of the family, making her own rules at a time when that simply wasn't done, at least not by women. Gert's husband worked for the railroad, and, as she received discounted tickets, off she'd go—alone—when she pleased. She was a Christian Scientist, too, another rarity in the South, and compounding all this unorthodoxy, before she married my grandfather, she'd played piano in a honky-tonk.

"Is that true?" I remember asking, as a young girl.

"She's a Christian Scientist," my mother said, as if that were proof enough.

I loved to hear stories, and Gert loved to tell them. She often claimed she was descended from a titled line of French royalty, though by all other accounts she was a native of Michigan City, Indiana, which was its own story.

Her home was filled with radios, one in nearly every room, perhaps for the connection they provided to the wide world she longed to explore.

Like the radio, her life was full of music and stories and other worlds, and I channeled a bit of that peregrinating spirit as I ventured across the United States in search of a library. We sought help from Great Dane Trucking, based in Savannah, which graciously offered to send a truck and trailer up to New York, and not long after, I found myself in other strange places, like Charleston, West Virginia, to comb through the stacks in their enormous public library facilities, looking for unwanted treasures.

Steven and I also showed up at postal auctions, where items that had never been retrieved from various post offices around the country were up for sale at extremely reduced prices, and we picked out every relevant volume on art, design, history, literature, you name it. We chose some just because they were ornate.

We hauled used bookshelves into the old ballroom, and my father built new ones, and pretty soon, we had what was starting to look like a library. But the work wasn't done. The books had yet to be classified, organized. We'd barely had time to go through everything.

"And it's ugly," I said one day to Steven.

"What's ugly?"

"The whole room."

I wanted our library to be beautiful, special.

"Are libraries supposed to be beautiful?" he asked. "Seems like all the ones I've seen were sort of—bare."

There it was again—the comparisons to others I'd heard before, the skepticism, the doubt. *This is not how other colleges do it. Other colleges had endowments. Other colleges had donors.*

Other colleges had millions of dollars and were old and crusty. Other colleges weren't us.

"This is an art college," I said. "Our students are studying beauty, and they deserve a beautiful library."

My two grandmothers had been lovely, singular women, but when I thought about grace and beauty, I thought only of a woman who was a grandmother to me in every way but biologically: Jessie Corinne Ward Fleming.

We called her Rinnie. She was born in North Carolina, but by the time I came to know her in my childhood, she owned the house on Lawton Street in Atlanta. Though she had a son, he lived in Albany, Georgia, which in those days seemed far away. My parents became her surrogate children, I her adopted grandchild.

She was loving to me, doting and kind, sewing all my recital dresses, letting me choose the fabric I liked best, the lace and the buttons and the trims. I remember a white organza tea-length dress with a gathered and scalloped edge that Rinnie had lovingly topped with pale pink rosettes. I wore it to as many recitals as I could, until it was much too short and the hem had begun to fray. She finally managed, in her gentle way, to coax me into releasing this fading beauty, replacing it with a new dress, just as lovely.

I was devoted to her, and she was kind enough to carry me along when running errands and on adventures downtown. "Lady adventures," she called them, during which we had tea at the Frances Virginia Tea Room, or lunch at the S&W Cafeteria, or else we window-shopped, me trying to match her light, neat steps, swinging my little purse as we went along.

In the years since, I've come to see how the old and the very young share a kinship, facing one another from the opposite ends of life, both nearer to heaven than those struggling through the middle years. She was my first friend, my dearest confidante, keeping secrets about the treasured buttons and seashells I had hidden in my sock drawer and how I'd managed to go to bed without getting caught for not brushing my teeth.

"I won't tell a soul," she'd say, smiling.

She set a beautiful table, with Easterling silver she kept in a cherrywood chest, wrapped in royal blue felt, with which I practiced my apprenticeship, polishing each iced-beverage spoon and salad fork every Saturday afternoon. There was a certain propriety in it, a decorum and rectitude in the way she fashioned both her home and herself.

She lived in an old Victorian, with a mansard roof and twelve-foot ceilings and saltcellars in every nook and cranny. Once a week, the produce man would bring his truck by; he weighed each item on his little scale while Rinnie told him what she needed for the week's menu. In summers, she made tomato aspic, serving the chilled jellies with deviled eggs and asparagus on china, and in winters, she served Russian tea, the leaves mulled with cinnamon and cloves and citrus juices. She passed on the recipe to me, and I make it in the late fall and winter, carrying the white ceramic pot into my office, snug in its cozy, sharing it with guests. Its aroma is a memory. Rinnie stays with me still.

Every child should feel she's the most special in the world, and Rinnie lavished her attentions on me. Thirty years later, I'd want our students to feel the same way—loved and cared for. After all, weren't we teaching them to see all the beauty in the world, the way Rinnie had taught me?

As I stood in the midst of the towers of unshelved books, I felt her presence all around me. Rinnie. She would want this place to be beautiful, too.

...

"A mural," I said to Steven. "We'll put a mural on the floor."

I commissioned Larry Connatser, a local self-taught artist, to design and paint the entire floor of the ballroom in a book motif. Larry also created the painting we used for the first catalog cover, while Steven designed the college's crest, the bee and the acorn representing industry and strength. Truly, from the very beginning, the whole look of SCAD was fashioned with beauty in mind, inspired and created by artists and designers and writers.

When I came across an especially apt passage by John Ruskin—"Fine art is that in which the head, the hand, and the heart of man go together"—I knew this captured something essential about what we were teaching students, this marriage of the intellectual, the malleable, the personal. We even created a vibrant logo illustrating this new college motto, which was later realized in brilliant neon.

We had most definitely used our heads, hands, and hearts to build that library.

By the fall—September 1980—it was ready for students.

The library quickly became much more than a home for books and a center for learning. It was also one of our first exhibition spaces. Here, the college held its first exhibition on loan from the Smithsonian, a show titled *Perfect in Her Place: Women at Work in Industrial America*—featuring photographs of women working in the late nineteenth and early twentieth centuries. We'd gotten the show to Savannah the same way we'd gotten the books—by asking. Politely. Persistently. Through letters and phone calls and the everlasting tonic of good manners and diligence.

"Did you bring the cookies?" Mom asked.

"Yes, Mother. And the exhibition catalogs."

She and I provided all of the food for the openings in those days, and vacuumed, and hung the work, and did just about everything else short of making the work ourselves, like the women before us, the women who made me: She and Olive and Gert and Rinnie.

"What do you think of the show?" I asked her, a few hours before the opening reception, after we'd finished vacuuming one last time.

"Oh, it's lovely," she said. "It's perfect. Women working. Look at them all."

We paused for a moment to enjoy the work together, before the crowd arrived, and then, without speaking, we both returned to our labors.

Chapter Six

Sidewalks

Savannah was a curious, lovely place, a city on the margins, at the edge of a continent, in between the New World and the Old, a safe place on a bluff on a river in the wilderness.

Within a decade of its founding, Savannah was home to the first Jewish congregation in the southern United States, with sizable communities of Salzburger Lutherans, Scots Presbyterians, Irish Catholics, and many, many others. Oglethorpe outlawed slavery, as well as the practice of law, at least for the first twenty years of the city's history; clearly he wanted the city to be distinct among colonial settlements. Where many early American cities were saturated with only a single Protestant denomination or a predominant ethnic group, Savannah was in between, a little bit of everything, an outlier.

And yet, nearly two hundred fifty years later—by the late 1970s—Savannah resembled a number of other old American cities, embattled with economic distress, urban decay, and a general flight from city centers. At night it was bleak, empty, menacing.

"Downtown will never be the same," longtime residents said. So many Southerners have always flirted with the romance of lost causes, but I liked to think the idea of a revivified city was not lost, an ideal shared by several of our new friends in Savannah, friends like Lee and Emma Adler, and A.J. and Kelly Cohen—friends who believed in SCAD and urged us to tell more people about our ambitious plans. In those first years, I found myself sitting with so many different community leaders, listening, trying to learn what the city needed. We sat in parlors, climbed City Hall stairs, looked across desks at movers, shakers, bankers, business owners, the great Mayor John Rousakis himself, where his office overlooked the wide brown river in which the city's founders had set anchor many years before.

By all accounts, Mayor John Rousakis was a character, tall and affable and determined to rejuvenate Savannah as a destination city, including his harebrained idea to bring tourism to River Street, which in the late seventies was Skid Row. He was a great teller of jokes, and many locals considered his visionary riverfront revitalization plan a joke, too. But if Savannah was going to have a future, I thought, it was going to be through visionary ideas like the mayor's. The mayor knew that Savannah needed more people, and we agreed. He wanted to bring tourists, which would bring business, while we wanted to bring students, which would bring whole new communities of residents, faculty, staff, and, of course, more business.

The mayor and SCAD had a lot in common, I thought.

"We need to go introduce ourselves," President Rowan suggested one day.

At the time, some in the community—really, very few—seemed to lump our students in with the criminal element, confusing outrageous hair with outrageous delinquency. There had already been efforts by this small minority of naysayers to block us from buying local properties, first the Armory and later a dilapidated rooming house we wanted to rehabilitate and turn into our first student residence.

"It's a historic home," this small clique of concerned citizens said. "Those art kids will just tear it up."

Those art kids.

Those art kids were bringing life back downtown, I wanted to say.

Those art kids were buying groceries, purchasing art supplies, and volunteering in local schools and hospitals.

"So, you're the folks who started that little art school?" people would say at cocktail parties, or when we were out around town, at the grocery store on Skidaway Island, shopping at Oglethorpe Mall. Faces and names came out of the woodwork, once word had gotten out that our little school wasn't going away.

Most long-standing Savannahians embraced SCAD. And yet a few local residents clearly did not understand the logic that would transform a historic downtown residence into contemporary student housing. Their thinking was, why take a dying property and reincarnate it into something it was never designed to be?

We thought Mayor Rousakis would see it differently.

President Rowan made some calls, got a meeting. He asked me to join him.

...

The mayor, red-faced and grinning, a wing of silver hair over his forehead, looked the part of a Southern politician. As soon as we set foot in his office, he and President Rowan started talking sports, a language I did not speak.

"So, what can I do for you?" he asked.

"We just wanted to tell you about our college," I said.

"Oh, yes, the little school that could!"

There it was again. Little. The look on his face suggested that he believed we were there for a favor, a handout, free buildings, something. We chatted about our students, our mission, our hope for the college and the city.

"Ah, yes," you could see him thinking. "Now it comes."

"Our mission," President Rowan explained, "is to prepare students for careers—"

"Careers?" the mayor said, cutting him off. "In art?"

"And design."

"I thought art students had those mohawk things," he said, "and the purple hair!"

He let out a great big laugh, I suppose, at the thought of sleepy little Savannah being overrun with punks and hipsters and revolutionaries, clashing with locals in seersucker or pearls.

"They don't all have purple hair," I said, handing him a catalog. "We have an unofficial motto: 'No more starving artists.' The mohawks are optional."

He smiled.

As we talked, I couldn't help but think of the city's many incongruities. Savannah was as free as its namesake river yet as buttoned-up as the preppiest good ol' boy, with all the festive liberalities of New Orleans and the hardworking conservatism of cities like Birmingham or Dallas. It was a town of parades and churches, equal parts playing and praying.

We had that same paradox in our growing body of students, young people who could have stepped out of Princeton or Yale, with their pressed khakis and polo shirts and penny loafers, and others with bandanas tied around kneecaps, ripped Levi's, and multiple piercings. It was the 1980s, after all, not the 1880s—whether or not some wanted to admit it. We wanted our students to know that they could fully express themselves on any canvas, including their bodies, but we also wanted them to find careers and professions, to land jobs. And so we had begun to teach students how to present themselves, how to prepare a portfolio, how to speak, listen, draft a letter, pitch a client, and do their elevator speech, which is exactly what we were doing there with the mayor.

"Thank you for seeing us," President Rowan said.

The mayor looked a little bewildered, maybe confused. Is that all we had wanted to do? Talk about our mission?

We left, and the mayor's chief of staff, whom we had met in the lobby, walked past us into the office. We weren't even out of earshot before the man asked Mayor Rousakis what it was we wanted.

"Not a damn thing, apparently," the mayor said, laughing that same big laugh.

...

The real objective of the meeting, of course, was to show him that we were here not to take, but to give. We brought resources to the city. At the time, there seemed to be an expectation that nonprofits, while they served a fundamental civic function, were also weak, pitiable, shaking tin cups in the street. Ours would not be one of those institutions.

In some ways, we wanted to be more like a purposeful cohort of inclusivity—a nonprofit, yes, but more than that—a community of doers and makers that added value to the city, brought stability, and created moments of meaning. Our students were nascent professionals.

How could we show this to Savannah, this heavenly city that had shown us such warmth, hospitality, and kindness? I wanted them to get to know the kind, talented, hardworking students who were helping make the city grow and shine again. How could they meet our students, not from afar, but in person, and see their work, their charm, and their gifts?

"We need an event," I said one night over dinner.

"We need money," Dad said. "Then we can have more events."

"Like an exhibition," I said. "But different." And then I saw it—all five hundred students, filling the squares, making art. "We're going to need chalk. Lots."

I asked Susie Clinard, one of our very first staff members—who'd go on to finish her degree at SCAD and become our first valedictorian—to work with me on it.

"Like, drawing on the sidewalk?" she asked.

"Yes."

"You're going to give chalk to students and let them draw on the street?"

"Yes."

"Shouldn't we get permission?"

"Probably."

I'd been reading about sidewalk art in Europe, and I talked it up to the faculty and the students, who loved the idea, which sounded so much like graffiti. The works were ephemeral, surprising, here and gone. There was something unexpected about it, this willingness to spend hours on a work of art that could be washed away with a single shower of rain.

At the local art-supply store, while my father winced, I wrote a check for enough chalk to cover every sidewalk in the Western hemisphere, which the store special-ordered for delivery on the day before the event, while Susie walked the sidewalk up and down Bull Street, praying for no rain and marking off concrete canvases for students.

"It'll be our first outdoor exhibition at SCAD," I announced to the students. "A sidewalk arts festival."

"You can woo some of the city's collectors," Susie said.

"Invite your friends," we said.

"Bring your parents down."

"Get out of the studio."

"Partner with a friend. Do something together."

"Two squares are better than one."

"And win a prize."

"A prize?" the students asked. Now we had their attention.

"A hundred dollars," we said.

The afternoon before the festival, clouds gathered.

"We should pray," Mom said.

She was our patron saint, a prayerful and faithful woman who never stopped believing someone or something was watching out for us.

"If we don't pray for SCAD, who will?" she'd say.

"What's the opposite of a rain dance?" Susie asked.

What if it rained? What if nobody came? What if the event drew the wrong kind of crowd, with rowdy drinking and revelry, and something happened that ended up in the news, in the paper, blamed on the students?

"See?" our detractors would say. "These art kids are trash."

It was a risk we would have to take. The local TV news had already announced the event, as had the paper. Everybody was coming, some to play, some just to see it all collapse, the way you can't look away from a traffic accident. We had high school art teachers heading down from Charleston and Atlanta with prospective students. What if nothing worked?

"What do we need to do?" I asked.

"Eat," Susie said. "When did we eat last?"

"It's been a few months."

We looked up at the sky, all except my mother, whose eyes were closed.

It rained. And it rained. And what it rained was people.

Madison Square was a carnival, families pouring over the sidewalks up and down Bull Street, more faces than I had ever seen in and around Preston Hall. I saw new friends from the community, kind and openhearted people I'd met at cocktail parties and city council hearings, and I saw many educators and students I'd met in art classrooms and at the art association meetings, as well as prospective families, teachers, and working artists. A riot of new friends, new faces. I saw guests in costume, children laughing, playing. I saw Savannah letting down its hair, and our students playing hard at their work. The street was one long unbroken canvas, eventually extending from Madison Square to Monterey Square four blocks south, a concrete quilt of what SCAD had become in only five years.

I didn't know it at the time, but a metaphor lived inside this new festival, a seed that would grow up through the garden of our little college and would touch every degree program, where the very rigor of the constraints compelled students to think in new ways. The students had limited space, about three feet by three feet, and an unforgiving surface with an unorthodox and volatile medium, and they had limited time, no more than four or five hours, to make their work. Many had brought along sketches, ideas, and concepts they had worked on ahead of time. They were learning to plan. Visitors asked students questions about their work, and the students stopped and stood up, engaged.

"Like professionals," I thought.

Many students had chosen to replicate their favorite paintings from art history, imitations of Klimt, Dalí, Rubens, Seurat. The rough chalk lent itself to impressionism and everything after, the blurred lines and explosions of color and light.

"You have to come see what this one student has done," Susie said. "She was complaining about her square. It had this big hole."

We walked over. Around the hole, the student had drawn a sunken ship, an underwater scene, and she'd lined the large hole in plastic wrap and filled it with water.

"Do you see what's in the hole?" Susie said.

"Is that a goldfish?" I asked.

"His name is Hieronymus Bosch," the student said.

A few squares down, a student had drawn the shadow of a parking meter as it fell across the concrete, then had redrawn the same shadow at intervals all day.

"Meter Descending a Staircase No. 2," the student said.

"Duchamp would love it," I said.

"I just wish I could keep it," he said.

There was a lesson there too. The students were learning to not hold on too tightly to their work. They were learning to move on, keep exploring. And so were we.

At the time, none of us could have known that the SCAD Sidewalk Arts Festival would go on to become the single largest annual outdoor arts event in Savannah, drawing fifty thousand guests. I'd conceived of it as a one-time event, an experiment, an early sketch to see if anything was there, as fleeting as chalk art, as unlikely as our new college.

Our first Sidewalk Arts Festival earned a brief mention in the *Savannah Morning News*. In the years since, it's been featured on ABC's *Good Morning America* and in *USA Today* and magazines around the world.

Sometimes people ask me, "How does the college get along so well with the city?"

The answer, I explain, has something to do with sidewalks and chalk and events that bring the city to our students, and our students to the city. I still remember that first festival, when, near the end of the day, I felt something on my shoulder. It wasn't rain. It was the mayor's hand.

"This is fantastic," he said.

"What do you think of all these crazy art kids?"

He smiled, laughed his great big laugh.

"I think we need more!" he said.

"We're working on that," I said.

Chapter Seven

Miracles

I sat on the floor of my office and wanted to laugh, scream, cry, run, although what I probably needed most was sleep. Marisa had already had her nap for the day, as had John Paul, our baby boy, just now learning to crawl. Hard to believe my daughter was nearly four and my son was already nine months old.

It was 1982, and all of us were on the floor, Marisa with her markers and coloring books and scissors and glue, intensely collaging, barely noticing that her little brother had begun to chew on one edge of her manila paper.

While Marisa made her collage, I made a collage, too, in words, cutting and editing and moving whole paragraphs to new pages, surrounded by my pens and pencils and binders and books and reams of paper. Goals linked to outcomes. Evidence. Lots of evidence.

I was preparing for what would be the most important moment in the history of our educational invention—the college's first accreditation visit by the Southern Association of Colleges and Schools Commission on Colleges, or for those who know it, simply SACSCOC, one of six regional accrediting bodies in the United States. (And reportedly the toughest.)

When we first opened our doors, SACSCOC had granted us provisional approval, with the promise of a full site visit and the need for a complete compendium of supporting evidence in a few years, and now those few years had passed. It was time. We needed their stamp of approval as a way to demonstrate to prospective students and their families that we were here to stay. Accreditation was important also because a failure to earn it would mean no federal financial aid for students, which would mean, in very little time, no students, and no SCAD.

I watched Marisa make her collage and considered how this act of creating was so similar to building SCAD. You take the bits you like, the ideas that make sense, carefully extract them from one context, and combine them in a new way, inside a new frame.

"What are you making?" I asked Marisa.

"I don't know yet," she said.

I surveyed the reports around me. We had hundreds of pages of evidence to submit, and it all fell to me, the academic dean.

What were we making here, at SCAD? And would I be able to explain it coherently in words? Failure to earn accreditation would be a death sentence, at least for a young institution with no endowment.

"How's it going?" came a voice from the doorway. My mother.

"What are you doing here?" I said.

"You're not the only one who works weekends."

She offered to take the children to get some lunch, for which I thanked her profusely.

"You should come with us."

"I can't."

"Think happy thoughts," she said.

"I can't."

"It can't be as bad as the authorization two years ago," she said, reading my mind.

"Sure it can."

"No," she said. "Nothing will ever be as bad as that."

She was referring to the most harrowing moment in all my years in education, when, two years before, in 1980, a team representing the Georgia Department of Education visited our brand-new little school. I sat there in my office, the shadows of leaves raking across the sun-dappled floor, the memory of that week raking across my mind, when everything had nearly come crashing down.

...

Back then, we had no graduates yet, we barely had students. We were young, and I suppose we enjoyed the overconfidence that youth affords. After all, three of the four founders had worked for the state or elsewhere as educators and administrators. I suppose we thought we knew the drill, but we did not know the drill. The drill was about to know us.

The official purpose of the visit was our need to be authorized by the state to award degrees, which was a requirement of all institutions of higher education in Georgia at the time. President Rowan, in fact, had worked at the Georgia Department of Education only a few years earlier and had helped draft the language of the very standards we would have to meet. His knowledge of the authorization process was key to our success here.

The team arrived on schedule—on a Monday in the spring of 1980—six reviewers in all. The spectrum of higher education was represented, with experienced arts faculty from a large research university, an elite liberal arts college, and a small but established art school. They had impressive credentials, and they wasted no time.

They asked about the mission, and we told them: It was focused on the students. On their professional careers. On individual attention. On being positive, encouraging. And we told them about our curriculum, with its foundations in classical arts education and the liberal arts.

The team seemed especially surprised at one fact about us.

"So none of you has actually taught at a university?" they asked.

What I wanted to say was, "So none of you has actually founded a university?"

But I didn't.

Of course.

My mother would never have forgiven it.

At every turn, down every corridor of the Armory, they seemed to be surprised at what they found. At the end of their first day on campus, they were invited by President Rowan to dinner at a nearby restaurant, a short walk from their hotel, and that's when the questions got pointed. But we were ready for anything. We had the whole team there, every key administrator—to answer questions about admission, finances, strategic planning. I was there to answer questions about curriculum, the faculty, the academic mission.

"So why did you do this?" they asked.

It was an unusual question, like asking why Kandinsky used so much blue. Because it was there. Because he could. Because it worked.

"Why?" I said, smiling, trying not to seem defensive. "Why not? More education is always a good thing. Don't you agree?"

They didn't smile back.

I tried to see the situation from their perspective. It wasn't the other SCAD team members present that they were concerned about—after all, our president had been an administrator at another university, had worked for the very office they were here to represent. And neither were they concerned about my parents, whose backgrounds made a kind of sense for finances and admission, my father having made a career in numbers, my mother having worked with educators, supervisors, and counselors for many years. No, it was me they were asking.

It was me they didn't understand.

To these men, sent to judge us, I was nothing more than the president's smiling wife, here to serve tea, but never, never to invent or administer curriculum. No, absolutely not. They called me the "chief cook and bottle washer" of SCAD. They laughed, and I smiled.

"It's just, your background seems rather unusual for this sort of work," they said.

I guess I could see it, how to them it must have seemed a twisted logic that could make an elementary school teacher think she could materialize from the ether and create the entire academic program for a new institution of higher education. What I tried to explain was that I'd done this before. I'd created my own curriculum once already. "It's not the first time I've written a curriculum from scratch," I said, telling them the story of Charlie Pepe and my educational experiments at Sarah Smith Elementary and other schools.

...

"I need you to do something for me," Charlie said during one lunch period, as we sat across from each other in the school cafeteria, where we chatted almost every day. This was before I'd ever had the idea to start an art school for children. "Don't you have some training in teaching gifted students?" he said.

"Yes," I said.

Practically my whole master's program was focused on gifted education.

He described what he needed me to do: take part in this new initiative across the school system to challenge the brightest students. They'd have to test into the class.

"What would I teach them?"

"Whatever you wanted to."

"Anything?" I said.

My heart was eager to say yes, before my mind could get itself around the concept.

A few months later, I was teaching one hundred fifty students every week from first through fifth grades. I wanted the students to use every talent they had, every gift. We made music. We painted. We designed. We took photographs and wrote and performed original plays.

When I was in my early teens, I'd enrolled in the Singer Sewing School, a nationwide summer program where students could learn to cut and sew a series of increasingly complex garments, from a silk blouse to a wool suit for a young lady, lined in the same silk as the blouse, every dart and seam and hem perfect, should anyone see the inside of the coat. (I still have the golden oval pins I earned from Singer, along with my piano-shaped pins from the North American Music Teachers Association, from years and years of memorizing and performing classical works.) These experiences taught me much about the effort it takes to make something beautiful and functional with your hands—and how to focus unflinchingly on a single object, to get every detail precisely right. I wanted my students to learn those lessons, too, and so I had them designing and cutting and making costumes for scripts and films we wrote and produced ourselves, shot on an old Super 8. We researched in depth, expanded traditional vocabulary lists, created entire productions. Our classroom became a multiuse learning space, part library, part workshop, part soundstage.

"Every child is an artist," Picasso so famously said. "The problem is how to remain an artist once we grow up."

I hadn't set out to make our class an arts-focused class; I merely followed my bliss, created my own curriculum of the best ideas I'd experienced as a teacher and student throughout my life.

High intelligence, as I was beginning to see in my students, usually meant high creativity. The two were not mutually exclusive—as conventional wisdom believed—with engineers and statisticians on one side, novelists and composers on the other, engaged in an intellectual tug-of-war. No, the most intellectually gifted people are creators in whatever venue they find themselves, inventing solutions for thorny problems. One thorny problem we had was scheduling, and how to get so many students into my class daily, without disrupting the other classrooms and teachers.

"Here's a new schedule," I said to Charlie one day at lunch.

"For you?"

"For the whole school."

I showed him how it worked, how it was the most efficient use of our space and the faculty's time. He took the schedule and half of my lunch and seemed pleased with both. I tried to carry on in my explanation of why the schedule was a good idea, how the schedule itself undergirded my detailed curriculum mapping and behavioral outcomes, but Charlie cut me off with his signature line.

"Darling," he boomed, "don't say another word."

It was his way of saying, "I get it, and I like it, so let's do it."

By the end of that first year of our scholastic experiment, owing to the freedoms afforded by Charlie's implicit trust in me, I'd created a literal school within a school, including an original curriculum, wheels within educational wheels of my own pattern. I kept waiting for him or someone from the head office to come check on what I was doing, but nobody ever did. No need for their interference, I supposed, especially if the parents were happy, and they seemed pretty happy, already lobbying for their students to get back into my program the following year.

Without anyone to tell me what sort of a job I was doing, I decided to create my own measurements. I developed pre-tests, post-tests, rubrics, and assessments for each major assignment, identifying clear criteria against which to measure student progress in every activity. I distributed these rubrics to the students. When they presented their book reports, they knew to make eye contact with their classmates and not fidget—because these requirements were written down on a dittoed piece of paper in everyone's hands. They were learning about more than books; they were learning the ancient art of rhetoric, the necessary skills of poise and wit and how to present themselves. Every few weeks, I asked the students to let me know how I was doing as their teacher—through anonymous feedback cards to gauge their reactions to my methodologies. If I got to assess them, why couldn't they assess me? It was a two-way street.

"To teach is to learn twice," my mother always said, and finally I understood.

Their joy was mine. They learned, I learned. We grew together.

...

These were the stories we told the visiting team from the Georgia Department of Education, sitting there at dinner, President

Rowan and the rest of our leadership team, trying to explain our philosophy of education, our policies, our vision for this tiny little art college in this small Southern town.

Our conversation lasted long into the night. We shared with them the college's desire to serve all students, to be somewhat unorthodox in our admissions, to seek students in unconventional places—homeschooled students, students interested in engineering and physics and literature as well as painting and illustration and photography.

"Many students don't know they have a gift for art and design," I said, "because they've never studied it. They've never been told it's okay, that one can have a career doing it."

"A career?" they said.

This word, I guess, was as uncouth to these educators as it was to everyone else. In 1980, it was taboo to discuss the word *career* while discussing a university education, unless you were talking about law or medicine. But art? No. That was no career.

"Why not?" I wanted to ask.

What I wanted to say was this: The clothes we're all wearing were designed, weren't they? The Armory was designed. The flooring, the photographs in the catalog, the curtains—created by artists and designers. They had gotten paid, hadn't they? They'd made a living at their work, hadn't they? But I didn't point out self-evident facts and observations. Cooler heads would prevail here, I felt.

The questions kept coming, the pens kept moving.

They wanted to know why we offered no classes on Fridays.

"For more individual attention," I said. "With professors."

They wanted to know why we met only ten weeks a quarter.

"So students can study fewer subjects in a more concentrated period of time," I said.

More jotting.

"Why's your mascot a bee?" they asked.

Was this a serious question? Did this really matter?

Everyone was getting impatient, my colleagues in the administration stepping in to help, to turn the line of questioning back to what mattered.

"No, I can explain," I said. "Bees love beautiful things. They love flowers. And they do something useful. They work industriously, together. They make honey. And they work hard. They never stop. They're diligent, collaborative, enterprising. And besides, they say the bumblebee shouldn't be able to fly, but it does, somehow. Just like us."

They kept pressing, baffled as to why we needed a mascot at all, since we were an art school. I was confused as to why it mattered. They were not here to accredit the mascot.

"Do you plan to offer athletics?" they said, almost with a laugh.

"Maybe," I said.

It didn't make sense to them, you could tell. An art college. Careers. Athletics. Nobody does this, they seemed to be saying.

Other colleges had classes on Fridays.

Other colleges had endowments.

Other colleges had tenure.

Tenure, that was a big one.

...

Nearly forty years ago, when the ivory tower was taller and virtually unassailable, the proposition of rejecting tenure was utterly alien. Revolutionary.

"But why?" the team wanted to know.

"For the students," President Rowan said, explaining that it was egalitarian, democratizing. No politics, no fiefdoms. Why be judged by titles? Why not be judged by your work? And not work from five or ten or thirty years ago, but recent work?

"SCAD is a student-centered institution," he said.

"Everything we do is for the students," I said.

In this, there was no compromising.

I compared it to work in any other profession—flying planes, building houses, conducting business—how the men and women in those areas were judged every day, every week, every year by their results, their work. Why not faculty members, too? Every quarter, every year, the faculty doing well would be recognized with contracts and merit increases. Those who were not doing well would receive help and feedback to improve.

"How will you identify who's not doing well?" they asked.

"Class observations," I said. "Student evaluations. Peer evaluations. Self-evaluations. Supervisor evaluations."

"And what happens if they don't improve?" they asked.

"Then it's time for them to move on," I said, "just like in any other profession."

That's what we meant by existing for the students. SCAD students deserved the best faculty, those who work hard every year, year after year.

At the time, in 1980, none of us knew how bad the adjunct situation would become in higher education, largely as a result of the tenure system. The college's rejection of the tenure model would prove itself an innovation when, thirty years later, we'd have an annual faculty retention rate that hovered around 95 or 96 percent. We simply wanted to create a system of accountability for everyone, staff and faculty.

"No tenure also means no teaching assistants," President Rowan reminded them.

Some large universities, then and now, stick many first-year and second-year undergraduate students into enormous lecture halls with one hundred, two hundred, six hundred seats, in lower-level survey courses taught by graduate students who don't yet hold a terminal degree. This was how these institutions could afford to pay tenured professors much more money to teach far fewer students. But why take the least-experienced teachers, often graduate students in their early or mid-twenties, and ask them to teach the institution's least-experienced students, only a few years younger? I understood the historic reasons for tenure, but in contemporary higher education, where employment constraints and protections apply to all staff and faculty members, it just didn't make sense. What made sense was having degreed, credentialed faculty members teach every class.

"Every class?"

"Every class," President Rowan said. "And no giant lecture classes either."

Even our general education courses—for example, the introductory surveys in art history—were taught by full professors.

"SCAD is a teaching institution," he explained. "Teaching matters most here."

The same principles that worked in my elementary school classrooms worked here.

You have to love your learners.

You have to have joy.

You have to layer the learning with project-based instruction.

You have to be accountable and prove what you've taught.

You have to move around, fight inertia. More field trips. More action. A teacher on her feet is worth two in the seat, as the saying goes.

And you have to give every student a fair shot at academic success, including both the students who come from the best high schools and those who don't.

"Every student starts with an A," I'd say to my elementary school students. "It's up to you to keep that A." Some of those students had never before earned an A, and they had begun believing they could never earn an A. I wanted to change that. I wanted to change their expectations of themselves, and I wanted to bring that same positive approach to SCAD.

"We've tried to be open minded about what's possible at a college," I told the visiting team. "Inclusivity. We think it will work. I've seen it work in my own classes, with my own students. I know it'll work here too."

I smiled while they jotted, and jotted, and kept jotting.

After three days of meetings, what felt like a lifetime's worth of inquisitions, we gathered at the Hilton Savannah DeSoto, one block north of Preston Hall, to hear the team's final decision.

We waited in the lobby. They'd be coming down any minute.

"I don't think they like us very much," I said to President Rowan and the others, our whole leadership team, including key faculty and administrators. Over the last hour, as afternoon classes let out, more and more of the SCAD family had gathered at the hotel, knowing something big was coming, waiting for news.

Time passed. An hour. Two hours.

"This feels bad," I said. "They really hated the no-tenure thing."

"They're just scared. They're threatened," Mom said. "We're young and fast and smart, and they know it. Higher education is changing. We have an advantage over every other institution out there."

"Please tell me what that advantage is," I said. I needed some encouragement.

"Youth," she said.

What irony, I thought, that one of our oldest employees—my dear mother, who, along with my father, was supposed to be enjoying a long and happy retirement—understood that SCAD's greatest asset was its youth.

And she was right. We were young. I was thirty-one years old now, surely the youngest academic dean at the youngest college in North America. We were too young to know even what rules we were breaking. We had no tradition to contend with, no history, no legacy. We were building from scratch, writing new rules. Their line of questioning wasn't about tenure. It was about our freedom to decide for ourselves what the character of our college would be.

Finally, one of the visiting team members was on his way toward us.

We stood.

"Well?" I asked.

"A question," the man said, looking very grave.

We waited.

"What if they deny you?" he said. "What will you do?"

"What do you mean, if?" President Rowan asked.

"They're considering denying approval," the man said. "What would you do if that happened?"

My mind ran wild with all the ramifications of a denial by the visiting team. How had this happened? All our materials and evidence were in order. We had made sure of that. We couldn't be denied—no, it wasn't possible. A denial would mean we'd be unable and unauthorized to operate or confer degrees. A denial would shut us down.

"They're not going to deny us," I said. "They can't."

"Sure they can," he said. "If they did, what would you all do?"

This man had been sent out of the room, I suppose, to test us, to see if we'd fight or not. The whole gathering of SCAD family looked quietly panicked, anxious. This was what we had feared. Would we blink? Would we fight? What would that mean? Legal action? Would we have to close our doors, default on our debt, lose it all?

We simply stared, unable to summon any words at all. Minutes, seeming like hours, ticked by. After a few uncomfortable moments, the man abruptly excused himself and whisked back up the elevator.

I wanted to chase after the man and apologize, tell him we would redo our reports, redo our assessments, gather new data, revise our mission, our curriculum, come up with new strategies, do anything and everything we could to save this place, whatever it took to keep this dream alive. We needed this approbation, because approval from the visiting team brought with it the authority to award degrees. If obtaining approval meant genuflecting to the bureaucrats at other colleges, then I was willing to do it.

But I couldn't run after him. All I could do was sit down, sink into the chair, and try to think beyond the hollow feeling of dread deep inside.

Who knows? Maybe it would work. Maybe they'd back down. Maybe they wanted to see if we actually believed in ourselves, our mission, all these wild ideas we'd discussed during their visit.

I stood up with my mother, took her hand, took my father's.

"It'll be fine," I said. "We can do this. Whatever they say, whatever happens, we can do this. It won't be over."

Thirty minutes later, the man came back downstairs.

We held our breath.

"You're approved," he said. "Congratulations."

Whatever we did, it worked. Maybe it was our stories, our joy in this work, our hearty defense of our academic programs. Maybe it was our stellar leadership team, with their passion and heart, or the knowledge and experience of our president.

Who knows?

But it worked.

...

That was in 1980.

Now it was 1982, and a different regional accrediting body was preparing to visit, and this one was larger, more thorough, demanding even more evidence and documentation. I sat on the floor of my office while my children played outside with their grandmother, and I tried not to think about the past, tried only to think about the future—that it would be better this time, that we wouldn't be subjected to another Grand Inquisition, a fearful inquest that felt deeply personal and threatened the very existence of the college.

"Here, we brought you some lunch," Mom said, coming through the door with two happy children, red-cheeked from their exertions in the park. We had grown a lot in two years. We had nearly five hundred students now, nearly thirty faculty members.

"Please tell me it won't be like the last authorization visit," I said.

"It won't."

"Good."

A few months later, SACSCOC visited the Armory, and after a thorough review of documentation and a site visit, they awarded accreditation to SCAD. We've been accredited by SACSCOC every day since. That first team, back in 1980, had expected to see a lot of marching to a universal university drummer. But SACSCOC, they got us. SACSCOC loved our perpetual quest to devise, design, improve, prepare, actively teach and learn, and evaluate our success—to do it all better while moving forward.

...

Around the same time we learned about our successful SACSCOC accreditation, I received a call from an Atlanta journalist curious about what we were doing down in Savannah.

"How large do you plan to grow?" he asked.

"We have five hundred students now," I said. "We'll have two thousand pretty soon."

"Wow," he said. "That's quite ambitious."

I don't know why I said it, or where I'd come up with that number. Now that we were accredited, we had nowhere to grow but up.

"Who was that?" Mom asked, after I'd gotten off the phone.

"*The Atlanta Weekly*," I said, referring to the Sunday magazine of the *Atlanta Journal-Constitution*. "Although I think maybe it was a prank."

When the story came out, we saw that it was no prank. There it was, right there in a magazine, our college, our dream, and the quote from me, explaining we would soon quadruple our size.

"You really said that?" she said, showing me the magazine.

"Oops," I said. "I guess we have to find fifteen hundred students."

The title of the article was "The Miracle on Madison Square."

I looked around at what we'd made, this building, this school, our library and classrooms and studios and talented students and faculty, this community, this family, this humming beehive. Those first five years had been wild and full of moments both harried and heady, and we'd done it. We'd made a new college.

And yes, it did sort of feel like a miracle.

Chapter Eight

Fires

Impressions linger from our first decade at SCAD—work, home, children, study abroad trips, recruiting across the nation, the world, commencements in the square, then in a church, then a bigger church, then in an auditorium, then the Savannah Civic Center, a voluminous cavern large enough for Elvis Presley and Elton John and us. We added dozens of new degree programs, in architecture and video art and more, as well as graduate programs. This was a big deal. We weren't just creating professional artists now; we were creating professors, too.

"I want to start referring to ourselves as a university," I announced to the communications team one day, now managed by my little sister, Pam, who'd spent years working in similar roles at other universities across the South before moving to Savannah.

"But we're not a university," one staff member said. "I mean, are we?"

By the late 1980s we offered more degree programs than most art schools, including the Master of Fine Arts—the highest degree attainable in most of the disciplines we taught.

As I explained all this, Pam nodded. She and I could have been twins. Not only were we of a similar height and build—both petite, low to the ground, like gymnasts, with bangs and earrings and an effortless laugh that most people could not tell apart—but we also thought each other's thoughts. Our minds melded; our spirits spoke a language others could not hear. Pam had the kindest eyes, always bright and smiling, and having her in Savannah brought a new light to my work and life.

"I think what she means," Pam said in the staff meeting, "is that we're not small anymore. We offer multiple degrees, including the highest degree awarded in most of those disciplines."

Yes, I wanted to say. *That's exactly it. That's exactly what I was thinking.*

"Right!" I said. "If we claim to be the best art school in the world, then we need to stop calling ourselves a *school* and call ourselves a *university*."

"Exactly," Pam said.

She got it, and she helped others get it through her work in communications so I could focus on working with faculty to design curricula and remarkable facilities and events that best showcased the work and talent of our students. In those days, most of what I did was behind the scenes, just beyond the limelight. That's what always felt most natural for me. I was all about the details, a writer of reports, a dotter of i's, crosser of t's.

I've always been this way, even back to my youth, when I played piano. I might've been performing in large competitions and recitals, but I preferred playing in the front parlor of my childhood home or my practice room in college, when I was alone. These quieter spaces were my truest stage, where I was my truest self. Only in quietude, I thought, could I do my best work. My piano teacher taught me the formula for success: exposition, development, recapitulation. But always, always, play with feeling, with heart, with artistic expression.

One of the great unexpected gifts of building the university from the ground up was that each of the four founders had been cast in the role best suited to his or her individual talents, even when that role wouldn't have made sense elsewhere. Where else could I, now the provost, also be lead designer for university facilities? On paper, it made no sense, but these were my gifts and where I flourished. If education can't let you shine, what can?

...

In those days, my office was full of faculty members and parents and students. I distinguished very little between my former work as an elementary school teacher and my current work as SCAD provost—it was about being a part of students' lives, for better or worse. The work required one to engage on a personal level, immediately, unceasingly, holding students' hands, listening, asking how I could help.

Take Will, for example.

I hadn't seen him much that fall, or winter, or even in spring of what should have been his senior year. He was rarely to be found at SCAD events or in studios or the wide hallways of the Armory. And then, one day in May as graduation approached, he suddenly appeared in my office.

"Provost Rowan, we have to talk," he said, in a panic. "I'm in so much trouble."

"Calm down," I said. "Whatever it is, we'll figure it out. Have a seat."

He sat unsteadily in the chair.

"I need a big favor," he said. "Like, a really big one."

In many ways, Will looked great. He had a fantastic tan and looked as vibrant and alive as a happy college student should, despite his shaking hands.

"Where've you been?" I asked. "I've seen you hardly at all this year."

"That's maybe the problem," he said, and then it all came rushing out of him, how he'd taken his parents' checks—meant for tuition, supplies, books—and squandered the money.

"On what?"

"I don't even know," he said. It didn't seem to be an intractable problem. I was certain we could get him back on track.

"We can get you back in class this summer," I said.

"There's something else," he said.

"What?"

"I have fourteen family members on their way to Savannah in a few days to see me graduate."

"Oh, Will."

"They don't know."

"Will."

"Could I just walk across the stage?" he asked.

"Not if your studies are incomplete."

"Well, could you maybe just print my name in the program?"

"Of course not," I said.

Deception, I reminded him, cannot be remedied by more deception. He collapsed back into the chair, defeated. He was quite sorry, I could tell. I suggested we call his parents and that he offer to get a job and repay the money, with the intent of reenrolling and actually completing his degree at a later date.

"Everyone makes mistakes, Will," I reminded him. "Loving parents forgive their children. Life is full of second chances."

People wondered what I did as provost. Was it all just writing curricula and faculty observations, creating new academic degree programs? Yes, it was all that, and also a lot of Wills.

I also spent a great deal of time working in admission. The light

I see in students' eyes when they first discover SCAD is unmatched by any star. Every day, prospective students and their families could be found peeking around corners in the Armory, and I gave many admission tours in between meetings. On one particular day, I hosted a mother and her son, Henry, as they explored the wonders of the grand old Armory. As Henry met students and professors busily absorbed in teaching and learning, he became more sure of his desire to study in the new video program at SCAD. He wanted to act, direct, and produce, and talked animatedly of starring in his own film.

"I sort of love it here," he said.

His mother, however, became more and more perturbed as we looked in on classes and discussed the curriculum. Finally, she asked to speak with me in private. Henry sat in on a class while she and I talked in the hallway.

"I truly want Henry to fulfill his God-given talent," she confided. "There's just one thing I can't see him ever doing."

"What's that?" I asked.

"I don't think I could allow him to take the life-drawing classes you mentioned," she said. "For religious reasons."

"I don't understand," I said.

"I saw some of the drawings in the hallway," she said, her voice dropping even lower. "And those women didn't have on any clothes."

"Oh."

"Henry has never seen anyone naked."

Right there in the hallway, while Henry was enraptured by the engaged learning experience in a nearby classroom, his mother and I ruminated over all the possibilities, finally deciding that perhaps his best option was to substitute mechanical drawing, which would involve no naked women of any kind, only naked architecture.

"That sounds perfect," she said.

Henry enrolled at SCAD and graduated—and after twenty-five years with Georgia Public Broadcasting, he has recently retired to life at the beach. But I can't avow that he never saw a naked woman.

This was my work, and I loved it.

Individual attention, it seemed, was the key to being a parent, professor, and provost. This is what I loved doing—creating solutions with and for students. What I didn't know, what I couldn't have known, was that all of us were about to be thrown into the middle of something that offered no conceivable solutions.

...

It started small, in the spring of 1992, and grew to something bigger than any of us.

In later years, after depositions, hearings, suits, countersuits—the legalities of which prevent me from using the names or identifying details of most of the involved parties—there was much disagreement about what actually happened, but this we knew: At the center were several malcontented faculty members and a few impressionable students who wanted to start a revolution, to create a sort of art happening that they would document on film, to what end, I never learned, perhaps to star in a film about conflict and conflagration.

Some said it started that spring when a group of graduate students petitioned for a student government association made up of themselves. Their proposal was denied simply because nothing about SCAD should be exclusionist. As provost, I applauded the students' desire to be engaged with their learning community, but I hoped they wouldn't be conformist, that student involvement would contribute to their development as emerging artists and designers. It just wasn't the SCAD way. When a student's petition was deferred, many became upset and began organizing protests. That's how some said it started.

Others, though, said it started earlier that spring with two or three faculty members whose contracts were in danger of not being renewed, owing to concerns about the quality of their instruction or other reasons. As provost, I made these difficult decisions, working closely with chairs and deans, reviewing observations and evaluations to determine which faculty members were deserving of salary increases and who might not be the best fit for our institution. In this particular case, in this particular year, all evidence pointed to the serious and immediate need for improvement in two or three departments.

These instructors were angry.

They knew they weren't being invited back to teach, and they wanted to strike out.

It was later suggested that one or two of these faculty members had worked themselves and those graduate students into a frenzy—some of the same students upset about a student government decision. These faculty members held meetings, confabbed in secret to contact the board, have the administration removed, piling up grievances they believed would somehow result in their being promoted to these vacant administrative positions.

What had begun as a rumble among the faculty and students soon grew into a roar.

Those of us who'd been at SCAD since the beginning had different reactions. Some of us were baffled, and some were angry—and rightly so—about how a few newly hired but voluble faculty members were using students' class time to soapbox, how they made fresh demands every day, and how none of this had anything to do with the mission and purpose of the institution. The ruckus was driven by the personalities of certain professors and students who wanted bigger roles. Much bigger roles. I'd been naïve to think that SCAD's most difficult years were behind us, because in an instant, it became clear: Our most difficult moments lay directly ahead, and there didn't seem to be a way around them.

...

I was in my office at Charlton Hall on Pulaski Square, a short walk from the Armory, when I saw the gathering congeries just across the street, under the oaks. It was dark outside, and I was trapped in the building, surrounded by a threatening crowd of gruesomely masked figures.

"What are they doing out there?" my assistant asked, standing in my office doorway.

"Is that fire?" I asked.

"What are they burning?"

We ran to a different window to get a better look, and there we saw it: the placards, the signs, the protesting, the flames, the smoke, the burning of figures in effigy.

"Is it an art protest?" my assistant asked.

We watched, we waited, we wondered. Then the yelling began.

They were chanting, demanding the president resign, that I step down, that the entire administration be tossed out. They were demanding it, as they jeered and cheered one another's taunts. They marched and yelled and declared their threats into the night air with well-orchestrated precision, chanting, demanding, I suppose, that we abandon our life and work, the only home we'd known for nearly fifteen years.

Security advised us to sit tight.

Eventually, the fire department came, but flames of misguided zeal could not be contained that easily. This small faction began to make noise, urging students not to register for summer or fall classes, condemning instructors who signed contracts for the next year, and going so far as to write letters to our lenders, suggesting we be foreclosed on. One of these disaffected faculty members even contacted SACSCOC, asking them to investigate us.

I stayed up nights, working with a small handful of dedicated professors to prove in the facts and the footnotes that we were in compliance with all accreditation criteria, and I stayed up nights with my children, who had been threatened with anonymous postcards and phone calls. I stayed up nights wondering which front of which battle was the real one. Bombs had gone off—placed around the administrative building—small ones, according to the investigators, but still dangerous, murderous.

I couldn't believe any of this was happening, and neither could most of my colleagues on the faculty and staff whose own livelihoods and families were being threatened. I was hurt, broken, disappointed that everything we'd built seemed in danger.

"What do we do?" I asked my parents one night.

"Take it to the Lord in prayer," my mother said, as she always did. She believed strongly that heaven had its eye on SCAD, that we were doing God's work here. We closed our eyes, and we prayed.

"We'll get through it," my father said.

"We have to rise above it," she said, taking my hand. "Rise above it."

This was her trademark counsel, a simple proposition with which she encouraged Pam and me throughout our lives, elegant, powerful words that sustained me through many difficult times, when the weight of travail threatened to drag me under.

...

Soon, the FBI was involved, and then on the eve of graduation, another bomb threat came, this one at the Savannah Civic Center, where we held commencement exercises. We had to cancel graduation, for the safety of our students. The chair of the board declared it. We could not chance anyone being harmed.

It would be a long time before we'd know exactly how it all happened, when the students who'd been at the center of the violence were found, arrested, jailed. It was awful, terrible, their lives ruined, all our lives changed, our university forever altered.

For the next year, our attentions were tied up in hearings, depositions, meetings to repair relationships, to prove ourselves, yet again, to our accreditors, to work with the board on putting out the small fires that had grown big and hot.

After hours of being deposed and hearing others under oath—listening to painful testimony, watching dozens of hours of videotape of furtive meetings among faculty and students and even community members who'd long held grudges against the institution—we finally learned the truth of that tumultuous season: The university had been the target of nothing less than a takeover by this small gang of disenfranchised faculty members. One had to admire their nerve and ambition. They had a solid plan. Really, they did. They'd planned to have our accreditation revoked, to have the core of the administration removed, to step in as interim administrators and eventually offer themselves as permanent replacements for the president, the provost, others.

It was a fight for the soul of SCAD, and it all boiled down to this: These faculty members, the few whose contracts were not being renewed, simply didn't like us. They didn't like that SCAD seemed too little like what they thought a university should look like, despite—or, more likely, because of—the fact that we were accredited, successful, thriving. These transient academics came from more conventional, typical college environments where interminable committee meetings were the norm and pontification was an art form.

Things weren't like that at SCAD. We didn't want a lot of pedantic bloviating. We wanted to be the kind of institution where a student could suggest a new major in fashion (glory be!) and the university paid attention. And we were. Glory be!

We were different, and they didn't like it.

All I could think about was how my mother had said, many years before, that everybody would want to be a part of SCAD once it was successful, that everybody—even naysayers—would want to get on board. She'd been right. Once people saw we were a success, that we had more than twelve hundred students and were growing beyond every expectation into an international university, that's when everybody pounced. Yes, they wanted to jump on the boat—and then throw us overboard.

Within a couple of years, it was over, and we were still in the boat, and the university was still afloat.

Our faculty had stood up, stood with us.

Our students had returned, reenrolled.

We presented our evidence to SACSCOC and they agreed that everything was in order. We never lost our accreditation. Never lost true friends.

As my spirit tried its hardest to rise, I did a great deal of reflecting. We had weathered the storm, but had we done it in the best way possible? The upheaval had thrown us to extremes. I turned inward, toward the quietude that had always served me well, focusing my attention on maintaining our accreditation.

"I'm ready to move on," I said one night, during dinner with the family.

"That's what you have to do," Mom said. "Rise above it."

Rise above it.

It sounded too easy.

And yet, while we celebrated the victory, it was bittersweet. Our spirits were broken, our hearts rent in two, our entire world charred and smoking, ravaged. I didn't know if SCAD would ever be the same, feel the same. Something was gone. I hoped we could find it again.

Masterpiece in Motion

Chapter Nine

Songs

The college was changing, everything was changing.

It was April 2000, when the board convened to make decisions, to cast a new vision for the future of SCAD, decisions that would reflect the institution's tremendous growth, our evolution from a regional art school to an international arts university. There would be changes, they said, and Pam sat with me while I waited to be called into the boardroom to hear what those changes were, what role I would play in the next season of my life.

"You should sit," my sister said, waiting with me.

"I can't."

"Then stand," she said.

"I can't do that either."

Pam was the family wit, always making those around her feel better, trying her best in that moment to make me smile because she knew I was anxious.

"They've been in there too long," I said.

"It's a board meeting. It's supposed to be long," Pam said.

"They may ask you to be president," Pam said. I was nervous, dizzy, feeling the way I did before a recital, when I could feel the anticipation in my hands, my fingers electrified, my body charged. "You'd be a great president," she said.

"I don't know," I said. "Think of all the speeches." Public appearances daunted me.

"If you can play a Steinway for a panel of judges and a full auditorium, you can handle the speeches," she said.

I'd started studying piano at the age of six and took lessons with Peggy Mayfield just up the street from my childhood home in

Atlanta. Soon I was competing in statewide competitions, earning ribbons, learning a lot about the virtue of practice, practice, practice. By high school, I was singing in the choir and accompanying every soloist on piano or organ, and playing Chopin, Mozart, and Haydn during regular performances for audiences as large as a thousand.

"That's all a speech is, anyway," Pam said. "It's your sheet music."

"We're putting the cart way before the horse," I said.

My parents—who had retired from their staff roles at the college and who now served on the board—came out of the meeting room.

"We recused ourselves," Mom said.

They sat down. They were tired. Both of them were over eighty but insisted on serving. The four of us sat there quietly, waiting, holding our breath. It was evening now, the board still convened, still hammering out the future of SCAD.

They called me in.

...

The reason for this meeting was that by the year 2000, the college had grown so much, so far beyond even our loftiest imaginings back when we'd first opened our doors with 71 students. By 1995, we had more than three thousand students, and we had earned more than a dozen national architecture and preservation awards, including the National Preservation Honor Award, the highest honor of the National Trust for Historic Preservation.

Savannah had rallied behind us too, showing us more support than ever. Philanthropists joined our board, while Georgia Governor Zell Miller had declared January 26, 1995, to be SCAD Day. Everyone from *The Wall Street Journal* to *Vogue* had written about the college.

In 1997, my parents retired, and to honor them we rechristened Preston Hall—the Armory, a building purchased, in part, with their life savings—renaming it Poetter Hall. In 1998, Tony Bennett performed a concert in our newest building, the old Weis Theater, now called Trustees Theater, on Broughton Street, an Art Moderne gem that would allow the university to start offering new degree programs in performing arts and to host large events, including the Savannah Film Festival, which we launched a year later.

By 2000, we had more than five thousand students and were accredited not only by SACSCOC but also by the National Architectural Accrediting Board.

We were soaring.

I had so many ideas, so much I wanted to do. I had big plans for our new film festival, big plans for Trustees Theater—to host a fashion show, to invite the biggest names in the industry to celebrate the work of students. It would be the biggest fashion show in the South.

SCAD had changed so much, and so had my personal life.

I had recently gone through a divorce, and my children were no longer babies. Marisa was now enrolled in the university's art history and fibers programs, preparing for graduate study in London, while John Paul was preparing to study finance at the University of Mississippi.

And now, at the dawn of the twenty-first century, here I sat, facing the Board of Trustees, waiting to hear their plans for the college, plans that would reflect our tremendous and unprecedented growth. The first two decades of SCAD had been the realization of what had seemed to many an impossible dream. What would the next two decades look like?

And here is what they said:

President Rowan, the only president in the entire twenty-two-year history of SCAD, would be promoted to the role of chancellor, assigned the task of traveling and fundraising on behalf of the college, while the daily operations and management of the institution would fall to the new president.

"In other words," the board chair said, "you."

"Me?" I said.

"We hope you'll do it," he said.

The years reeled across my heart like filmstrips.

I'd known this was a possibility, but it had never seemed real. Titles had never meant much to me; they were just words. All of us here worked hard, threw our backs and hearts and souls into the college, no matter what our business cards said we were. But now, being asked to serve as president, I was overcome.

President?

Really?

I looked into my heart and saw my mother and father and sister, and how they'd helped get me here, the years and moments blurring like the trees and farmhouses and fences seen from the backseat of a family car, the long roads woven across the landscape of my imagination, leading me to my grandmother's farm in Mississippi, to college in South Carolina, to a new life in Savannah, highways and country lanes and bridges over tidal marshes, the utility poles and their parabolic lines dipping, rising, dipping, like the days, weeks, years, the low moon running alongside the car like a distant traveling companion, always there, while I was a girl, a woman, a wife, a mother, a teacher, a dean, a provost.

And now—what? A college president?

I thought about what I'd been doing, about helping students, asking what's best for them, what they needed, listening. I thought about Pattie Dyson and Traci Haymans and Will, and a thousand students just like him, and about all the faculty and staff I'd hired over the years, about the events and facilities and degree programs we'd created together. About all the board members I'd come to know and love. Is that what being president would be like? Just more of it?

I knew there would be much about the job I probably wouldn't love.

I would have to speak with bankers, brokers, and attorneys.

I would have to be in the newspaper and the press releases.

For the first time in my life at the college, I would be the final word on every major decision. I could collaborate as I always had, of course. I could turn to Pam and others for counsel, sure, but at the end of the day, I would have to look in the mirror and live with the decisions I'd made.

It had been eight years since the upheaval of 1992, but those days still lingered in the minds of so many of us who lived through them. How were we different now? How could we prevent that sort of turmoil from happening again? How could we retain the camaraderie, the fraternity, the close relationships of our first years, while embracing the new reality of our size, our reach? Could I know every student? Could I befriend every faculty member?

These were my questions as the board awaited my answer.

I sat there, listening, thinking, praying.

And that's when it hit me.

I would not be going it alone.

Even the most memorable soloists are backed by a chorus or an orchestra, many human hearts all yearning for the same thing. And wasn't SCAD very much a song? And wasn't my own life very much a sort of musical, with ups and downs and tears and laughter?

I looked around the table at the Board of Trustees, and I gave them my answer.

Yes.

I would do it.

We would do it.

...

President Rowan—now Chancellor Rowan—had been the ideal president for our first decades. He was visionary, an excellent giver of speeches, declaring bold new plans, amiable and personable with the students and the community.

I would have to be a different kind of college president. The newness of SCAD had always allowed people to find roles best suited to their strengths, and who said that had to change now? I could be a college president who designed interiors, who conducted classroom observations, who created showcase events for students.

A few weeks after my inauguration in the spring of 2000, a faculty member stopped by my office with an idea. His name was Jeffrey DeVincent, a new professor who had come on board a couple of years before to help launch a degree program in media and performing arts.

"I've been reading your children's books," he said.

In the late nineties, I'd written several stories inspired by the My Travelship volumes of my youth, about the lives of children from Guatemala to Greenland to the bayous of Louisiana, collaborations with SCAD alumni, a perfect marriage of my love of literature, education, and illustration.

"It's about *Remember This*," he said. This was my children's book—illustrated by professor Julie Mueller-Brown—about Maria, a young Guatemalan girl who loses a precious amulet in the jungle. "I love the book, and I sort of have a crazy idea."

"Okay," I said. "We love crazy ideas."

"I want to put it on the stage."

"Like, a play?" I said. That wasn't so crazy. We had a new performance space. We had the story. It was the sanest idea I'd heard in a long time.

"And I want to take it to the largest experimental theater festival in the world."

"Oh," I said.

That was crazy.

Soon, Jeffrey and I were busy at work, adapting the book, auditioning actors, and sitting at my piano transcribing songs that were coming to me from somewhere. I'd started writing songs and one-act musicals for my students when I taught elementary school, but that had been decades before. I'd forgotten how much I reveled in the pure act of creation, the way time falls out of meter and the world opens up like a great Panopticon before you. What a joy, to create beautiful work with faculty members like Jeffrey and many others.

"Do other college presidents write musicals?" he asked.

"I don't know," I said. "Is that weird?"

Within a few weeks, Jeffrey and I decided we needed another act, and Jeffrey set about adapting another story of mine, *Perfectly Still*, about an Inuit boy on a quest across the tundra, into the second act of the show, which we'd titled *Journeys*. That name said something about the hero of each tale, but also about the college—how far we had come and how far we had yet to go.

"Where is this festival, by the way?" I asked.

"Scotland," he said. "The Edinburgh Festival Fringe." He explained that *Rosencrantz and Guildenstern Are Dead* had debuted there and that Anthony Hopkins, Emma Thompson, and Robin Williams had performed there.

"Are they really going to like a children's show?" I asked. This was one of my first big initiatives as president. I wanted our production to be a hit, not a sideshow.

"They have knife-throwers and fire-eaters and operas performed entirely in sign language," he said. "We'll fit right in."

We cast ten actors to play twenty roles and brought in musicians to help finish the music and perfect the songs. The students were beside themselves at the opportunity to travel overseas and perform at a festival where most students only dream of performing. Soon, a SCAD delegation landed on Scottish soil—including the cast, crew, board members, a small group of staff and faculty, and me. My memory of the week is a whir of crackling, sparkling energy, the very ground vibrating with the hum of the human spirit. The show was flawless.

The next day, *The Scotsman*, one of the country's oldest daily newspapers, raved about the production, praising the actors for their discipline, the perfection of rhythm, the tightness of the blocking and movement, everything. Not long after, we did it again, turning two more of my children's tales—*Treasure True* and *Bayou Boys*—into *Journeys II*, a two-act show that played at the Kennedy Center.

These experiences showed me what was possible in this new era of SCAD. New degree programs could be discovered, new faculty leadership could be cultivated, and new art could be shared with new audiences around the world, if we only had the will to make it happen, to build it together.

As president, I could lead that effort.

Together, we could make a symphony.

Not long after we returned from Scotland in 2000, Chancellor Rowan resigned from his position, and I stood alone as the last of the four cofounders still working full time at the university. I was a single mother now, but surrounded by family.

What I felt for the past transformed from grief to melancholy, for what we had been, for what we had lost, for the storms my family and I had endured together. And now, I sat down at my piano to write a song, a hymn for SCAD. I received great input from Jeffrey and other colleagues about the song, and pretty soon we had a new alma mater for the university: "Unique, United."

A real university, I decided, should have a defining mission, an aspirational but realizable vision, high values, and most especially, a song in its heart. We could do anything. We could sing. We could soar.

"Rise above it," Mom always said.

It wasn't easy, but we did it.

All of us at SCAD rose together.

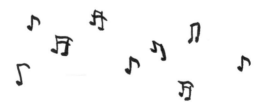

"Unique, United"

Through all our days
We will remember this
Community
Of excellence which is
Drawn from the Muses
And each continent
Unique, united
Masterpiece in motion.

Many are one
Converged through love of art
The head, the hand
And certainly the heart.
Now face to face
And then in memory
Unique, united
Masterpiece in motion.

Vision and courage
To surmount the tests
That come with joys,
With challenges and quests,
Here taught and learned
A circle without end
Unique, united
Masterpiece in motion.

Founded in faith
That it would be the best
A global family
That has been blessed
Built for today
And for those yet to come
Unique, united
Masterpiece in motion.
Unique, united
Masterpiece in motion.

Chapter Ten

Deeds

Not very long ago, I received a letter, addressed in cursive in the unmistakable hand of a child.

"How long have you been president of a college?" the letter asked.

It was written by a junior high school student who was researching careers for a project and decided being a college president sounded fun. I had to think for a second. How long had I been in this role?

I looked at the calendar.

Fifteen years?

That couldn't be right.

I recently read that the median term of service for a college president is just over eight years, although the record for the longest tenure of a president is sixty years, a record I'm not sure I can break without new technologies in human longevity.

I was thirty years old when I helped create SCAD.

I was fifty-one years old when I became president.

I've just turned sixty-seven.

Yet, most days, I feel like a little girl sitting at the piano in Peggy Mayfield's parlor, the same age as the young student who wrote me this letter, asking what it was like to be a college president.

I held that letter and thought a lot about the strange and wondrous places my heart had brought me: to Savannah, to the Armory, to the students, to the close friends I'd made at the university. In all my decades at SCAD, my heart had become bound to other hearts, those of faculty, staff, alumni, donors, and board members who believed in our work and our mission, even when others scoffed, laughed, and didn't believe.

One of those hearts belongs to a man named W.W. Law, a kindred spirit who taught me that the heart can do what the mind cannot conceive.

I liked him from the very first—and not just because he was vertically challenged, like me. He had many admirable qualities: intelligence, charm, oratorical power. He might've been short, but in every other way he was larger than life.

We shared a love for education and history. He'd grown up in Savannah, lost his father at age nine, stood in Roosevelt's breadlines, volunteered with the Army Air Forces during the Second World War, supported his aging mother while working as a postman, taught Sunday school, and found himself elected president of the Savannah chapter of the NAACP while still a young man.

"There were some who didn't want me to be president," he said. "I didn't have the right background, they said. I wasn't supposed to be a leader." And I told him: I also knew something about people saying I didn't have the right background.

It was W.W. who led the integration of Savannah's public schools, sit-ins at Woolworth's, wade-ins at Tybee Beach; somehow he'd managed to do it without the violence and unrest happening elsewhere, in places like Birmingham and Memphis and Jackson, during that tortured American age.

When he hadn't the time to sit and visit, he wrote letters, and in a world where the art of letter writing has all but vanished, finding W.W.'s notes in my mailbox was a rare pleasure. Many of our conversations and letters concerned how best to elucidate the African American experience in Savannah's history, a neglected chapter in the story of our city. I wanted SCAD to play a role in telling that story, but didn't know how.

"Your heart will tell you how," he wrote.

In 1988, the school board auctioned off four abandoned schoolhouses, and the college placed a collective bid on all four—buildings that would eventually become homes for the SCAD School of Foundation Studies, School of Fashion, and fibers department.

"There's another building you ought to put in a bid for," W.W. said.

He was referring to the Beach Institute, built in 1867 for the education of newly freed slaves, named for Alfred Beach, editor of *Scientific American*, who donated funds for the site. The building had been abandoned for nearly seventy years, and W.W. envisioned it as an African American museum and cultural center.

"You're buying four schoolhouses," W.W. said. "Maybe you get a fifth one for free."

What sort of nonprofit makes such a large donation to another nonprofit? We had already reinvested so much of our budget back into SCAD facilities that many guests assumed we were a for-profit institution. Would this gift to rebuild the Beach Institute only reinforce the myth that, due to our success, we were a for-profit entity? Did it matter? Wasn't the fact that somebody needed to help the only thing that mattered?

My heart told me it was right.

We added the Beach Institute building to the bid—and won. Immediately, we donated the facility to the King-Tisdell Cottage Foundation, of which W.W. was president. Later, we contributed labor to the restoration of the property, sending the university's craftsmen and artisans to help remake this cultural landmark.

My friend had let his light shine in the city, using his gifts to make it better, fairer, building lasting friendships across class and race and property lines, and I wanted our young college to do the same for Savannah.

"Use what God gave you," W.W. was always saying.

Twelve years after SCAD donated the Beach Institute building to the King-Tisdell Cottage Foundation, when I became president, I continued looking for ways to help the university's light shine, and I soon found a primeval wilderness very much in need of that light.

...

In the first year of my presidency, I teamed up with one of the great American artists of the past hundred years, Benny Andrews, to work on a new children's book, *Treasure True*, the tale of a young Gullah girl who lived on Sapelo Island, a place accessible only by boat or plane. On a research trip during the writing of the book, I was given a tour of this curious island by my friend Willie Mae Robinson, a member of the Savannah Arts Commission who'd grown up on Sapelo. She led me along from Nannygoat Beach to the island's famous Toothache Tree, and finally we arrived at a little church deep in the forest. Here, the First African Baptist Church at Raccoon Bluff sat in deep suffering.

"The congregation organized in 1866," Willie Mae said. "Right after the emancipation."

The church building was constructed in the first decade of the twentieth century from driftwood washed up onto the beach by hurricanes. By 2000, the church appeared as if it had suffered a hundred storms, its clapboards buckling, its windows blackened with mold and age.

"My people met here for seventy years," Willie Mae said. "All descended from Gullah Geechee slaves right here. They fished here, farmed here."

In the sixties, residents were thrown off their land, forced to abandon the church, their houses burnt or destroyed, everything cleared to make way for a hunting reserve. The owner of the land back then, she said, was tobacco king R.J. Reynolds Jr. It seems beyond belief that something like this could happen in our nation in the twentieth century, but it happened, an entire relocation of a community over something as trifling as a quail hunt.

Over time, the old First African Baptist Church building deteriorated, its tin roof rusted away, its white paint faded and peeled. Wasps had redecorated its walls with mud and nests. The property, which once belonged to former slaves and their descendants, was eventually sold to the Georgia Department of Natural Resources.

"The state says we can't have it back, either," Willie Mae said.

In all our years in Savannah, we'd learned a great deal about historic preservation and the rehabilitation of vernacular architecture. Surely, we could bring our resources to help.

"What can we do?" I said.

"Let's go inside," she said, "and see if we can see God."

Standing in the crumbling sanctuary felt like holding vigil at a deathbed—any moment could be her last, the violet and gold glass windows like luminous eyes struggling not to close, finally and forever. Willie Mae and I stood there in the shadowy, high-ceilinged room, illumined by the pale light streaming in where it could.

"I see my mother standing in that choir loft," she said, and began to sing "Precious Lord, Take My Hand," a hymn I knew well. I joined in, and together we sang of weathering storms, of dark vales of night, and waiting with hope for the light.

Later that day, Willie Mae introduced me to a lifelong member of the church, Cornelia Bailey, and I vowed to both women, as foolhardy as I must have sounded, that I would do everything I could to convince the state of Georgia to return the land on which the church stood, though I had no idea how I could make that reversal of fate and fortune happen.

...

I called Georgia Governor Roy Barnes.

He wasn't available.

And we tried again.

And again.

He was a busy man, and I called every day, then I had my assistant call, since she sounded different.

She tried for a few weeks.

"He's not available," she said.

"Keep trying," I said.

And then one day, he answered.

"Governor!" I said. "It's you! It's really you!"

"How is my favorite art school doing?" he asked.

I didn't waste time. SCAD wanted to help restore this old church, I explained, and we thought, as partners, the state might consider giving the land back to the church.

"You have the power to do this," I said.

He wanted to help, but the legal picture was grim, he said. It would take too long, would be contested, surely, by his political opponents. He apologized, promised to visit the next time he was in Savannah, and that was it.

That day, I walked into the office of Bob Dickensheets, who was both a professor of historic preservation and our on-call preservation expert. Bob was full of curiosity and kindness and knowledge about the built environment and its past. You could see why students loved him. You could tell by the way he touched a wall that he knew what was under it, behind it, what human lives had been poured into it.

"Bob," I said, "I was just down on Sapelo Island."

He knew what was there, the stories, the history. I told him about the church.

"You got to see it?" he said.

"I'm worried, Bob. The next hurricane will wipe their church off the map."

A few weeks later, Bob was on a ferry to the island, and he came back with a look that was both haunted and hopeful.

"We have to show our students," he said.

...

While the state of Georgia had not granted the church property back to the residents, it was generous enough to give us permission to begin restoring the dilapidated structure. The work was not easy. The site had no electricity, so power tools had to be charged by a generator, and without running water, construction workers had to carry buckets back to the site from the island's fire truck.

And then there were the insects—mosquitoes, biting gnats, spiders. "Spiders big as tennis balls," Bob said one day, showing me around. "One of them shook his fist at us."

The students, of course, loved it.

In higher education, the subjects of architectural history and historic preservation can sometimes edge perilously close to collapsing into mere theory. But with the First African Baptist Church and other projects like it, our students were able to see firsthand what it took to preserve and rehabilitate a historic structure—from conducting ethnographic research to interviewing island residents about past uses of the site to matching authentic paint colors.

Bob guided students in their restoration of the church's pine floorboards and its stunning stained glass windows, and in the removal and replacement of huge hand-hewn support beams that had been ravaged by termites. Bob's sons aided their father in rebuilding the fallen steeple from scratch, creating the technical drawing themselves and ferrying over the materials.

Despite roughing it, students came and kept coming. Most drove down on Friday mornings—the university had long ago decided we'd have no Friday classes, so that students could have more time, in part, for field experiences just like these—and many students stayed through the weekend for campouts, loath to miss a moment of the action. When Bob was solo, he quite happily stayed in a trailer that I'm sure a wild boar would've deemed too primitive, even though I offered to put him in a room on the mainland.

Bob soon paid a visit to the Hog Hammock Committee, an ad hoc city council for the island, and suggested its members send some of their children over to the construction site for a once-in-a-lifetime educational adventure. Soon, a whole cadre of children sat there watching, mesmerized, as hammers pounded and drills whizzed, and Bob walked them around the site, explaining how our SCAD team was bringing the building back to life.

Through their research, the historic preservation students found that the stained glass windows, though lovely, had been originally installed backward.

"Do you want them put in the right way?" Bob asked the Sapelo residents. "Or backward, like before?"

"Like before," they said.

And that's what we did. Our team brought in everything, not just new pews, but a new piano, new lighting, and four striking chandeliers that we had found at a flea market and that would suit the church perfectly, another piece of the puzzle, another sign that all this was meant to be. We even managed to find a nineteenth-century bell to hang in the steeple. When Bob tugged and it rang its clarion call across sea and land, we knew we were hearing God.

The rededication took place on a cold December day, nine months after I had joined Willie Mae in poignant, hopeful song. A troop of us arrived for the dedication ceremony via ferry, arms buckling under the weight of garlands, wreaths, coolers, and all the coats, mittens, hats, and scarves we could find. In the Georgia Lowcountry, we're not used to freezing temperatures, and it had begun to sleet and snow. I'd invited Governor Barnes, but we'd heard nothing certain in recent days.

"He's not coming," I told Bob, while we carried food baskets through the piney woods over the bluff.

"Too bad," he said. "We have enough fried chicken to feed the state legislature."

Dinner on the grounds is a tradition for Southern church dedications, and we'd hired a wonderful caterer, Susan Mason, to help with food. As we were unloading, Susan suddenly jumped back on the ferry as it pushed off.

Three hours later, I spotted a little boat crossing the river. It was Susan, waving.

"I forgot the cheese straws!" she said, her face chapped and red. "You can't have a dinner on the grounds without cheese straws. What if the governor comes?"

"He's not coming," I said.

Then we heard the helicopter.

The governor!

"I've got a surprise for you," he said as soon as he hit the ground, but he was rushed away by his handlers toward the TV cameras. The whole island arrived in Sunday best, as did media and faculty and staff and students who'd contributed to the work.

A small brass band in the choir alcove played "When the Saints Go Marching In" as the gas lamps glimmered along new walls. Then all the attendees stood to sing "Surely the Presence of the Lord Is in This Place," the first hymn sung by a congregation in this sanctuary in forty years.

Governor Barnes gave a speech, concluding his remarks by calling forward William Banks, a senior deacon, to stand beside him. Under the small black-and-white sign that read "F.A.B. Church, organized May 2, 1866," the governor delivered into the deacon's hands the deed to the land upon which the church stands.

...

Later, as everyone was sitting down to lunch, Governor Barnes approached me.

"Paula," he said. "This is absolutely the most moving event I've ever participated in."

A great many blessings came out of this experience, especially the idea to create more projects for students to join together, collaborate across majors with congregations or corporate brands or communities. Projects like these, I thought, showed students what real-world expectations looked like. Clients must be heard, deadlines met, work completed. Intentions evolve into meaning.

Our creation of the SCAD Collaborative Learning Center was inspired, in part, by what happened on Sapelo Island, the magic made between the students and the community, under the direction of dedicated, energetic faculty with extensive professional experience.

Not long after, we redoubled our efforts to give students opportunities to work with Habitat for Humanity and many other worthwhile causes, including traveling to the Mississippi Gulf Coast during school breaks after Hurricane Katrina to assess damage to historic structures. Closer to home, the university has continued to play a big role in bringing goodness and beauty to my beloved adopted city, such as our work a few years ago with Savannah's first arts magnet charter school for K–8 students, the Esther F. Garrison School of Visual and Performing Arts. In just under five days, before it opened, the SCAD family descended on the school to paint corridors, install lighting, hang new art on loan until the students could create their own, stock the library with more than one thousand art and design books that SCAD was no longer using, set up new computers and study tables, and create new landscaping, including a *grande allée* of palms leading to the front doors.

When I think about everything SCAD has been able to do for its communities around the world, from the Beach Institute to the First African Baptist Church to the Garrison School and beyond, I always remember the words of my dear departed friend W.W. Law, who was in attendance that day on Sapelo Island.

I was honored to see my treasured friend there in the church, slower with age, but no less full of vitality. After the ceremony, I found W.W., took his hand.

"You inspired this, Dr. Law," I said. "You know that, right? You did this."

"No, ma'am," he said. "I just showed you how."

Chapter Eleven

Loves

I was on Liberty Street, walking our dog, a little whippet who bounced gaily over the cobblestones like a dancer, when several young people with a map and bewildered looks stopped me to ask for directions. It was early September, and they appeared to be first-year students, owing to their look of enthusiastic and bright-eyed bafflement.

"We're looking for SCAD," a young man said.

I explained that the campus existed across the whole city. "It's not like other colleges and universities," I said. "It's everywhere."

"You must be a teacher," they said.

"Sort of."

"What do you teach?"

"I'm the president," I said.

"Of, like, the whole college?"

I gave them the inside track on when to start a double major and how to use their electives to add a minor and how working at the university's tea room, Gryphon, was a great way to meet visiting artists.

"Here's my email," I said. "Stay in touch."

Being president, I'd found, was fundamentally no different from being a teacher. The classroom was larger, that was all.

It was easy to love elementary school students, of course—students who were quick with hugs and who needed help tying their shoes—but SCAD students were just as precious, in many ways just as earnest, creative, and open to all the beauty and possibility around them. In them I saw the glorious paradox of the young artist. They were confident, competent, professional, but also vulnerable, sharing their fears and hopes with the world.

I wanted to provide an environment where students could learn to be resilient, hardworking professionals, but also an environment that was nurturing, where students were treated with kindness. That meant finding more great teachers and keeping them. One idea I had early on was to award fellowships to faculty members who had creative or research projects. Another idea was to make individualized help sessions a requirement in every class, to help prepare students for midterms, final projects, client presentations.

I wrote these ideas everywhere, and my staff found them in odd places, tucked between the pages of books, underneath teacups.

"Is this a note, or just scribbling?" they'd ask.

"Both?" I'd say.

"This one says something about trees and light."

"Maybe we need more trees," I said.

"Maybe you were sleep-writing again."

"I was dreaming of cypresses."

"Do you want us to plant trees?"

"Van Gogh's cypresses."

"You want us to plant van Gogh's cypresses?"

"I want to take students to see them," I said.

I scribbled everything on the backs of paper tea doilies, many of which I still have, notes about how to grow our new film festival (*screenwriting competition, master classes*), ideas for showcasing the design disciplines (*SCAD fashion week? Design week? Style week?*), ideas for new degree programs (*designing objects—cars, toys, something on the computer/online—ask students*). I still have many of these notes. They remind me that big accomplishments grow from small ideas.

...

Being president was about more than thinking up new ideas; it was also about building a team to help make those ideas happen.

A few years before becoming president, I'd formed Design Group to help me manage our many physical resource projects, and now that I was overseeing the management of the entire institution, Design Group needed a new director. I was already working closely with interior design alumna Alison Hopton, our offices overwhelmed with blueprints, swatches, photos, colors, ideas ripped from magazines.

"We need a new manager for all this work," I said.

"What about Glenn?" Alison said.

"Glenn Wallace?" I asked.

I'd hired Glenn a few years earlier to help us redesign and rehabilitate one of the university's historic properties for a contemporary academic purpose. I knew him well, had worked with him for several years already. He had many gifts in design and management. He was the obvious choice to work alongside me as the new leader of Design Group.

"Oh, he's totally the guy," Alison said. "You make a great design team. You're always dreaming up these wild ideas that seem impossible. He's one of the few people around here who can handle your curveballs."

She was right. Glenn wasn't afraid to poke fun at me when I had some crazy idea, like placing antique mannequins on a stairway landing or spiraling old hardback books around load-bearing columns, and then he'd find a way to make it work. We had a good dynamic, our ideas—like those books—spiraling around one another.

Glenn was promoted from project manager to director and principal of Design Group and soon we were spending even more time together. He'd worked in a family heating and air-conditioning business and seemed to know just about everything about what was possible in a building, structurally, aesthetically. He was inventive and immediately entrepreneurial.

"Let's hang this fibers sculpture right here," I'd say.

"What are we hanging it on?" he'd say.

"The ceiling."

"The ceiling won't hold that."

"Hang it on something else, then."

"Like what?" he'd say. "The clouds? A flying unicorn?"

"Sure."

"Okay, let me see if we have a unicorn."

Invariably, Glenn would figure out a way to hang the work, always coming up with an innovative solution that surprised with its beauty, its elegance. I'm the starry-eyed idealist, he's the pragmatic realist—but we had the same taste about almost everything, colors and styles and fashions and even families. It didn't hurt that he was stunningly handsome, a true gentleman.

"He's sort of perfect," I remember thinking one day out of the blue, feeling like a schoolgirl, all butterflies and rainbows.

A few weeks later, a group of us were at a design conference in Miami when we passed a fortune-teller in the street. Somebody suggested we all have our fortunes read. She read everybody's, including mine. Glenn was last.

"You will fall in love with someone who has hazel eyes," she told him.

"I don't know anyone with hazel eyes," he said, laughing.

I stood beside him, blinking my hazel eyes.

Sometime after, I finally summoned the courage to tell him how I felt, this man who loved dogs and children and cooking, who was strong and smart and funny and gorgeous—a man who loved holding hands, who prized his family above all else.

He felt the same way, he said.

"But the thing you said to the fortune-teller," I said. "About hazel eyes."

He laughed.

"I had to keep you guessing," he said.

We were married at Bethesda Chapel on Thanksgiving Day.

...

Our time together—at work, at home, in the car—was all so familiar, so comfortable. I shared with Glenn every secret hope I had in my heart, including something I'd been carrying with me for many years, as far back as my childhood, when I held my baby sister in my arms for the very first time.

I wanted to adopt.

It wasn't that I longed for something my family couldn't provide—no, the very opposite. The more love I gave to my first daughter and son, the more it seemed I had to give. When a family's working right, I think, that's what happens. Love seeks love, love begets love.

When I was a schoolteacher, I can remember watching students running across the playground, and thinking: *How could I love any children, even my sons and daughters, more than I love these children?* They were young, full of love and hungry to know. The memory of one particular student has stayed with me for many years, a boy of eight or nine called Antonio. He was quiet, healthy, happy, curious. One day in class, I noticed that he had an infected cut on his hand.

"What happened?" I asked.

"Nothing," Antonio said.

I cleaned the wound, bandaged it, and worried that perhaps his mother hadn't known the extent of his injury, which was nearly in need of stitches. The next day, Antonio was back, but the bandage was now sullied with dirt and ash.

"What happened?" I asked.

He shrugged. I dressed his hand again and applied a salve, and I did this every day for several weeks. I sent letters home to his mother letting her know how much I appreciated her son and how much I cared for him and his success in school, but I never received an answer back.

I was beginning to worry. Was he abused, neglected? Antonio was one of nineteen students in a second-grade class where I'd set a goal of taking each student on individual field trips over the course of the year. We planned Saturday trips to the movies, the zoo, the ice cream parlor. In letters home to Antonio's mother, I asked if she had any ideas for what Antonio might like to do on his one-on-one field trip, but again, no response. I noticed Antonio had quite an appetite, which gave me an idea.

"Would you like to make cookies?" I asked. "And then we could make lunch?"

"Okay," he said.

The day for our visit came. Antonio lived in a distant part of town, a long drive. When I got to his address, I thought there'd been a mistake. It was more of a shed than a home, leaning in the wind, barely the size of a garage. Inside, Antonio's mother was kind and gracious, but I couldn't take my eyes off the dirt floor and the open fire in the middle of the room, right there in the floor. No wonder the bandage was dirty and black every morning. Then, when it was time to go, I asked Antonio's mother to sign the permission form for our little adventure.

She quickly scrawled an X on the form.

That's why she hadn't answered my letters. She couldn't read them. My heart broke.

How could I love one child any more or less than any other child, a child like Antonio or a hundred others just like him? His mother clearly loved him—but what of the children without families to care for them? For many years, I'd felt called to adopt, and now, with Glenn by my side, the calling grew too urgent to ignore. Could we do this?

Glenn didn't need convincing. His own younger sister had been adopted into his family when she was only days old. He'd grown up in a family that knew the meaning of love. And that's how we found ourselves waiting at the airport to meet a little girl we named Madison.

...

She was two years old when she arrived. All of her words were in Mandarin.

"Madison," I said, saying her name to her for the first time.

"Madison," she said.

I held her close, hugged her tight.

On the day we brought her home, I sat in the back with her while Glenn drove. She looked with curiosity out the window at the passing marsh and tall pines, new sights in what would be her new home, studying them.

"Tree," I said, as we drove home, Savannah's geography providing the syllabus for Madison's first words in English.

Cloud. Grass. River. Island. Ocean.

We took walks along the marsh, talking, singing. I pointed, said the name of the thing, and she repeated.

"Mailbox," I said.

"No," she said, walking up to it, pointing at the numbers.

"Three," I said. "Three one two."

"Three one two," she said. "One two three."

"That's right."

The world of nature and numbers taught Madison her second language.

Soon, we took her to a toy store to pick out anything she wanted. Glenn would pull something off the shelf and hand it to her, and she'd stare at it.

"Show her what it does," I'd say, and Glenn would wind up the toy, set it on the floor.

Madison would stare and then place the toy back on the shelf—the lowest shelf, the one she could reach.

"Ooh, look!" I said, when we came to a full aisle of dolls. "So pretty."

I took some off the shelf, set them down on the floor in front of her. Even then, she insisted on walking, and I placed the dolls at eye level, so she could select her favorite. She reached out, touched them, touched their faces, their hair, put them back.

This continued, aisle after aisle, toy after toy, puzzles, games, stuffed animals. She'd study them, return them to the shelf. After an hour, we only had one item, something she'd taken off the shelf and held and not put back. A red rubber ball, the simplest toy in the store.

"She likes the ball," he said.

"Do you want the ball?"

She smiled.

"Maybe we should get her a bunch of them?" Glenn said. "We could build a ball pit."

But she just wanted the one.

She was strong, and yet tender, precious, the most peaceful, serene child I'd ever seen. I looked in the backseat, on the way home, and watched her looking out the window, holding on to that red rubber ball.

...

It was a blessing to see Glenn be a father. He had a gift for it, didn't carry with him any leaden baggage about what a father was "supposed" to be. His love for design, building, and making translated into his being a very hands-on parent. He had many great male role models in his life, including his wonderful father, Glenn Sr., and I knew he wanted to share that father-son bond with his own child, too, a third Glenn.

We prayed about it, talked about, decided to do it.

"Glenn Eugene Wallace III," I said. "I like it. What will we call him? Trip? Trey?"

"Trace," Glenn said.

We met Trace in our fourth year of marriage, and though he was only two years old, he'd already fallen in love with Peking opera, as evidenced by the very large collection of DVDs he treasured. The way some children watch Bible song sing-alongs or Bugs Bunny or Dora the Explorer videos, Trace couldn't get enough of

Women Generals of the Yang Family, *Monkey King*, and *Three Attacks on Zhu Village*.

As far as we could tell, his first word in English was *DVD*.

"DVD," he would say that first week, to Glenn, who sat up with him at night, his little finger poking into the air.

"Why's he poking like that?" I said.

"The DVD hole," Glenn said.

"DVD!" Trace said, shaking the crib.

As he got older, Trace grew to love the magic of performance even more. Madison and Glenn and I would laugh while Trace stuffed napkins into his sleeves and performed a bird dance at the dinner table, and when Marisa and John Paul were home for the holidays and school breaks, they enjoyed this young new breath of life in our home.

I couldn't help but think his love of Chinese opera afforded Trace a link to the culture of his birth, that there'd never be a day when he wouldn't know his roots, his beginnings. Glenn and I worked hard to give Madison and Trace stability, joy, a home that was theirs, sacred, inviolable, but we also wanted to ensure that they knew their own cultural histories.

When she was very young, Madison took lessons in Mandarin. I hoped that the language would never leave her, keeping the door to her past and to China open. I was perhaps too conscious of her heritage, in part because I was always being made aware of it by others, who asked, without ceasing:

"Where's she from?"

"Is she yours?"

"She looks Thai."

"No, Indonesian."

"No, no, no, Chinese."

I smiled, Madison smiled. It happened most often at the nail salon. The staff, always quite fulsome, was unafraid to ask.

Madison listened, soaking it all in as she had with the words and syntax of every language she explored, Mandarin, English,

Spanish, French, on her way to being the first one-member Model United Nations. Trace was still very young, but we knew he was full of his own surprises and talents, just like my first three children, who'd blessed me in countless ways. This is what rocks the soul, this vision of eternity one sees in children, the unbroken circle.

In Marisa, I see my love of literature and history, a talent for reading the subtext in any environment, any exchange. Unlike me, she is a gifted athlete, but we share an abiding intuition, the ability to follow our instincts when others urge us onto a different path, feeling our way with the mind and heart through a moment, a decision. She possesses a rare gift for communicating with animals, horses, dogs, all creation. She speaks a language others cannot.

In John Paul, I see my own fondness for working behind the scenes, a love of quiet preparation; while others are crowding the spotlight, he'll be in the back of the room, taking it all in. And yet, I've never seen a person with such a gift for gaining new friends without even trying, largely a result of his ability to listen attentively, his loyalty, looking people in the eye with genuine interest. And he's a sartorial dresser with impeccable taste.

In Madison, I see laser-like focus, an unfailing conscientiousness about her studies, her assignments, her family, her responsibilities. She doesn't require the sword of Damocles over her head to prepare for a test—often, by the time Glenn and I mention working on a class project, she's already completed it. She's deeply maternal, too, toward her younger brother, protecting and looking out for him, always.

In Trace, I see pure joy and energy, a playfulness that draws a crowd. I'm no extrovert like him, but I think we share a love for the imagination, for making, building, creating. We both love spectacle, the surprise of color and movement and shape in physical space. He's never in a bad mood—a gift more of us need to possess. When he was eight years old, he broke his arm and never lost the smile on his face. The first night in his cast, he sang himself to sleep.

...

Sometimes, I wonder if I've allowed my children to be their best, truest selves, to find their own purposes and callings, while I'm still on my own journey. This question has made me think a lot lately about what children need, what we all need.

After several years of taking Mandarin, Madison began to change, pushing away from these language studies.

"I want you to know where you come from," I said.

"I know, but—"

I could see it in her eyes, something growing, an awareness of what she was and wasn't.

"I want you to know your heritage," I said.

"But you are my family," she said. "You are my heritage."

I was rocked. I saw that what Madison needed, like all children, even more than immersion in her native language, was a family. All those times when people asked who she was and where she was from and who her mother was, she was paying attention to my answers, and my answers were wrong.

When I said, "She's from China," she was paying attention.

"I'm from here," she said. "You are my people."

"I'm sorry," I said. "I'm sorry."

It happened again on occasion.

"Where's she from?" they asked.

"Savannah," I said. "She's my daughter."

Madison smiled, almost imperceptibly. I watched her in the chair, reading *Great Expectations*, as content as that little girl so long ago in the backseat, holding a red rubber ball. I'd spent my life as a teacher and a mother trying to anticipate the needs of children. I thought I had a gift for it, and sometimes I did. But I learned, too, that sometimes what children and students need is simpler, right there in the mirror.

Sometimes, all they want is a red rubber ball.

Sometimes, all they really need is you.

Chapter Twelve

Travels

The dawning of the twenty-first century opened my eyes to a new life, a new way of being in the world. I'd learned to listen to the quiet vibrations of my heart, which led me to my best self as a mother, daughter, wife, sister, educator. My family was everything, which was why the news we received that day in 2001 took the very breath from my body.

"Your father has cancer," Mom said, while Pam and I sat with her one Sunday afternoon. Dad was napping, out of earshot. "He didn't know how to tell you."

No man lives forever, but Paul Poetter had confounded the machinations of time and death. He'd won every athletic record in track and field, swimming, and tennis in the city of Atlanta. He'd led his high school basketball team to more than one championship game, not to mention that football scholarship he'd been offered before the war. He'd served his country, and sailed over oceans, then retired, and unretired, donated his life savings to his daughter's dream, launched a new career in higher education. He encouraged students from the front row at every SCAD sporting event, and he was the loudest cheerleader, the jovial father figure, the ageless man in the blazer. He took more risks in his old age than most do in a lifetime.

"Pancreatic," Mom said. "They said three months."

"Daddy," Pam said, running to him after he woke up.

"It's fine, it's fine," he said.

"Three months?" I asked. "They just say that. They don't know."

Three months later, he was gone.

In the days after his funeral, I tried to measure what he'd done, how far we'd come because of him. When he moved to Savannah, our college was only a college on paper, with a budget of a few thousand dollars. The year he died, the university had a budget of one hundred million dollars.

I still remember fondly our squabbles over the cost of long-distance calls and easels and modeling clay. My father cared about the money because he cared about the mission.

"As long as it's for the students," he'd say. "Then I approve."

Any financial strength we had was and remains a direct result of his habits, his legacy, his philanthropy. As my mother often said, he was a man who would give the shirt off his back.

We mourned, a fogbank of grief hanging about our lives through Christmas, and the New Year, and the long, dark winter. My father had been the rock on which we'd moored ourselves, and now my soul was adrift.

"What will we do?" I asked Glenn, one wet February day, the cobbles of the city streets slick and marrow-cold.

"We'll do what we've always done," he said, taking my hand.

...

My father's death brought me to a crossroads, a time for questions, decisions. Who were we, what should we become? The college was blessed with surging enrollment across programs and departments, thanks to a leadership team that wasn't afraid to throw the tired conventions of higher education out the window if need be. We recruited determined and ambitious students in unconventional places: AP physics classes, homeschool debate competitions, high school literary festivals. We created our own guesthouse, Magnolia Hall, and restaurant, Gryphon, to conserve resources and curate the guest experience, to expand the professional friendship circle of SCAD. We developed shopSCAD, selling original work by students, alumni, and faculty. Many of these ideas came to fruition because of my collaboration with Glenn. We'd be sourcing materials for SCAD interiors and find ourselves wanting things nobody else wanted, broken cuckoo clocks, fragments of decommissioned carnival rides, discarded treasures of every color and kind.

"We need these," he'd say, digging through bins at the back of a secondhand store in rural Georgia, where we'd found seven or eight fiberglass Art Nouveau skulls.

"What you going to do with them old heads?" the owner would say.

"I have no idea," Glenn would say. "She'll think of something."

"Eight heads are better than one," I'd say.

And we'd throw them in the trunk, and a month later, they'd be hanging from the ceiling at some event, in the foyer of a classroom building, assembled in a nook at Magnolia Hall.

What is SCAD?

SCAD is taking an unfinished person, a broken thing, and seeing its beauty.

SCAD is surprise, the unexpected.

When would our next unexpected idea come?

Glenn said it was up to me.

"You're the boss," he'd say.

I wanted to know what the students wanted. I hosted teas for them at my home, in my office. We talked. I listened.

"What do you need?" I asked them.

"Help with my homework," they said.

"More time in the day," they said.

"Vegetarian options," they said.

I spoke to a number of students who'd participated in our off-campus study programs in San Francisco, New York, London, Paris. Something was different about these students, something in their eyes that came alive.

"I had a real breakthrough," they said.

"It changed my work."

"Travel changed me."

Change, breakthrough, travel. I kept hearing these words.

"We should be more international," I said to Pam. We'd always thought of ourselves as small, local, Southern. We wanted to be the finest art school in the South, but we'd blinked and found the world had come to us, as had the world's letters—from chambers of commerce and the offices of mayors of cities in Florida, North Carolina, Texas, New Mexico, California, and cities farther afield, in England, Italy, India, Singapore.

"We love what you've done for Savannah," they said.

The writers had scouted us out. They'd seen our students, our facilities, how we'd helped transform the city from a sleepy Southern town into an international arts destination. They wanted some of that magic in their own communities.

The university had been international from the very beginning, when faculty and staff including Jeff Eley, Craig Stevens, Tom Fischer, Josh Yu, Robin Williams, and many others took students to England, Italy, France, Canada, Thailand, Japan, Hong Kong, Beijing, Shanghai. I was privileged to join many of these traveling bands of happy artists and designers and educators, watching students gaze in ecstatic wonder as Lew Tate, who taught Shakespeare, walked with them through the Globe Theatre and told them the history of the place. And I stood with students outside Buckingham Palace on the day Princess Diana died, as they turned their cameras toward history. And I saw students come alive on the Spanish Steps in Rome, where Craig showed them how the design created a pleasing perspective linking the Piazza di Spagna below and the Trinità dei Monti above.

Fashion professor Ben Morris, my dear friend, once led a trip to Venice, asking his students to sit along the edge of the canals and work on their drawings. One of his students was working meticulously in colored pencil and marker but was growing frustrated. He had made too many errors, and eventually tossed his work into the water.

Ben fished out the wet drawing, its colors bleeding, and persuaded the student to keep working. The result was a phenomenal creation that was eventually framed and exhibited in the annual off-campus show. Sure, students can get frustrated anywhere, but there's nothing quite like having work shaped by Venetian waters. As Mark Twain wrote during his own Grand Tour in 1867, "I travel to learn."

SCAD was all about learning, and I knew we should take students to even more places that could teach them understanding, compassion, the language of the human heart.

...

"I just had an interesting phone call," Bob Dickensheets said one day. An alumna, he said, called to see if someone from SCAD might want to visit a tiny school in the south of France. "They need a preservationist," he said. "Roofs caving in, that sort of thing. They're looking for someone to come in and partner with them."

"Partner how?"

"They're looking for an American university that knows about historic preservation."

I knew a school like that.

But would this partnership be temporary or long lasting, like those ancient stones? Helping out the First African Baptist Church or historic properties damaged by Hurricane Katrina was one thing—flying across the world to help a French art school was something else.

Soon, Bob was on a plane to the Luberon Valley, to a place called the Lacoste School of the Arts, and two weeks later he was back, with pictures.

"They want to give us something," he said.

"What?"

"Their school."

"The whole thing?"

"Didn't you say our students should be spending more time abroad?"

The small school began in 1970 after American sculptor Bernard Pfriem bought a little cottage in Lacoste, a tiny village on a hill east of Avignon. Under Pfriem's direction, the school attracted many highly regarded artists to teach, from Henri Cartier-Bresson to Nene Humphrey. But Pfriem died, and the school had begun to struggle financially. By the time its board members reached out to us, they were determined to hand over the reins to another organization rather than watch Pfriem's school perish. They'd seen and heard what we'd done with historic buildings in Savannah. Granted, our buildings were only a century or two old, while according to Bob, this school had caves.

"*Caves*?"

"Dating back to Roman rule," he said.

"Rome?" I said. "Like, *Rome* Rome?"

"Like Julius Caesar Rome," Bob said. "Like aqueducts Rome."

I spoke often with the school's board chair, Nancy Herstand, an arts management and fundraising consultant from Miami. Nancy and I spoke the same language. She cared about students, knew what a gem this campus in Lacoste was, and saw something in our university that could save it.

I sought the advice of many—the executive cabinet, my staff, my mother, Glenn, Pam—but there was a voice missing, the one I felt I needed most: my father's. What would he say about this? Here was our chance to be truly international.

"Is this for the students?" I could hear him asking.

Was it?

Did SCAD need to stay small and local, or be something else?

A few days after commencement in 2002, I was on a plane to find the answer.

...

I love traveling because I finally have time to read. I groped through my bag and found a book, *The Letters of Vincent van Gogh*. Any armchair art historian knows the story of Vincent and Provence, his flight out of Delft and Paris on an old, bone-rattling train to Arles, not far from Lacoste. I read how the city had suffocated him, how he was searching for a breakthrough, and found it in Provence—in the sun. In a year's time, he'd painted nearly three hundred of the most important works in the history of humankind.

I jotted notes in the margins.

> *Learning to see.*
> *Light, color.*
> *Change.*

I looked at small reproductions of van Gogh's work from his time in Provence, where straight lines weren't straight, where colors were exaggerated, where he had turned his attention in odd directions, where a mulberry tree looked like a burning bush of scarlet, its boughs and branches curled in flame, the cypresses like cones of black smoke in the mistral, where human forms curved like pillars of fire and every star in a sky full of them had a distinct personality. The book grew heavy, and I napped, dreaming of students like a sky full of stars, each one unique, different.

...

In the car, powering up the valley with Glenn and Bob, the color woke me up, everything deeper, richer, saturated.

"My goodness," I said. "The light!"

"I know," Bob said. "The wind blows down from the Alps and clears the sky—no clouds, no water in the air. It's so pure."

"You know some French, right?" I asked Bob.

"The only French word I know is Chevrolet," he said.

Words didn't seem to matter as much when I finally saw Lacoste rising out of the surrounding orchards, brilliant greens and browns giving way to the whites and yellows of the stone houses and old medieval fortress walls in the sun. Their pink and red terra-cotta roofs comingled with the bluest sky, and rising out of it all was the renowned Château du Marquis de Sade, a castle that would become the home of international designer Pierre Cardin.

We climbed the cobbled streets, met representatives of the school, who walked us around the village, their properties, all of them in need of serious love and attention.

"This is bad," Glenn said.

While I spoke with school administrators, Glenn and Bob wound their way through the tiny spaces, around corners, poking, prodding, making notes, two surgeons looking over a patient. Could we really send fifty or a hundred students across the Atlantic to this place? Could we call it SCAD?

We stepped out onto a terrace at the top of the village, and the clear alpine air blew away every question, leaving nothing but beauty and wonder and a Roman road winding through the valley, where poets and artists had come in search of something. I contemplated Cézanne, Monet, Picasso painting the looming Mont Ventoux. Then, on a winding road, we passed a large, dilapidated structure at the base of the mountain.

"What's that?" I asked.

"The Maison Basse," they said. "The former stables of the Marquis de Sade."

"What is it now?"

"Nothing. Rubble."

Two of the board members bought it for the school, they said, but they could do nothing with it. They had no funds and only a handful of students. Not enough to warrant the extensive rehabilitation that would be required. I looked west, to the vineyard-blanketed valley where van Gogh worked, and to the southeast, the countryside of Aix-en-Provence, where Cézanne spent his most fruitful years.

They had come here to see something new.

Would I?

...

What does it mean to be a leader, president of what was on its way to becoming the largest nonprofit arts university in the country? If I had to sum it up in a word, it'd be this:

Decisions.

Lots of them.

Some take weeks, months to make.

Some must be made in an instant.

You gather all the information you can, get the right people in the room—somebody with a calculator, the brick-and-mortar people, the subject matter experts you trust, the faculty members you've known for decades—but at the end of the day, it's just information they're feeding you, for you are the maker of decisions.

"Well," says one.

"And of course," says another.

"But then..."

"And if you..."

"And if we..."

"Yes, if."

Some were worried, felt that the Lacoste campus would be a drain on resources. It's a money pit, they said. To them, resources were a zero-sum game, where you rob Peter to pay Paul. "We only have so much in the budget," one department chair said. Her feeling was, if you put money into something in France, you have to take it away from something in Savannah. Which was true, to a point, but seemed shortsighted, because, as others said, a new campus would attract new students who might not have otherwise considered SCAD, growing resources for everyone.

"You've got to go see it," I explained. "And we have to send students."

I told everyone what I'd seen, how merging with this small school could give our students permanent access to an international study experience, the opportunity to see themselves and their work transformed. To not just travel abroad, but live in a medieval village for a term. To collect memories for a lifetime. I let my heart speak where my head could not. The board of the Lacoste School of the Arts wanted us to take control of their properties. I made my case to the university's Board of Trustees, and they voted.

We would do it.

"What will we call it?" I asked Glenn, while we celebrated.

"EuroSCAD?" he said.

...

Glenn and I soon learned that contractors in France aren't that different from those in the United States—the electrician meticulous, the plumber often late, the painter fond of overcharging. We had a field day with these old structures, ranging through the architectural history of Southern Europe from the twelfth to the fifteenth to the nineteenth centuries.

And the caves!

The village sits on the side of a mountain of limestone, with natural crevices and veins carrying water, caverns in every other building, water running down the walls in winter, right through the classrooms. We solved the water issue, then set to work transforming one of the oldest structures in town into a Mac lab, perhaps the only computer lab in the history of American higher education housed in a medieval fortress. We wrangled with bats and cats and owls and the scorpions, families of them, small, mostly harmless, but nonetheless alarming, that lived in the caves.

So we added Internet to our caves and subtracted the scorpions.

Students and faculty arrived, new ones every quarter from Savannah, while we worked. Our rehabilitation of the academic spaces was slow, meticulous, labored, reliant upon the grant money we received annually through foundations affiliated with the former school. And when a grant arrived from the William T. Hillman Foundation, we were refueled for our largest and most extensive project yet, the restoration of the stables at the foot of the village, the Maison Basse.

The Maison Basse was a near-total ruin, a compound of five structures with no plumbing and little electricity, broken windows, collapsed stairwells. This was no armory in need of a good sweeping and a coat of paint. The Maison Basse had no roof. Another brilliant SCAD preservationist, Kate Firebaugh, took the lead, starting with the roof, once a hayloft, a tree pushing through what remained of it.

Kate and the other preservationists did phenomenal, mind-blowing work, and during each visit I helped wax furniture, hang art, haul books to the new library. Later, our students jumped into the project, too, working with us to execute commissions by artists Patrick Dougherty and Patrick Blanc. We constructed a pool at the Maison Basse, and the students jumped into that, too.

As our years of restoration work were just beginning, I described the village's stony lanes to André Leon Talley, SCAD trustee and *Vogue* editor who'd joined the board a year or two before. He'd lived in Paris for a while and had visited this area often. He knew it well.

"What should we call this place?" I asked.

"You must retain the SCAD name," he said. "It's too memorable to toss aside."

"But we can't just call it SCAD."

"SCAD Lacoste," he said.

It was easy: the perfect marriage of both schools, both places.

...

It's hard to believe that I first set my eyes on Lacoste more than a decade ago, to know that more than three thousand SCAD students have studied in this little kingdom on a hill, taking courses in illustration, painting, sculpture, performing arts, writing, animation, and every other degree program we offer, on rotation.

I try to visit at least once a year, to observe classes, contribute to the ongoing restoration work. Glenn and I like to rent a car and scoot around, hitting as many flea markets across Provence as we can in a day or two, unearthing treasures we have used at every university location, lamps and chests and dress forms and old theater props. We hold a vernissage of student work at the end of each quarter, and join students for jaunts to Paris or nearby villages in the Luberon. Back in Lacoste, I sit with students, to learn what moves them, what breakthroughs they're making.

"My work has never had so much color," they say. "Everything I made used to be gray."

"The light!" they say.

"The air!"

They wander the village, enlivened, exhausted from hours at the canvas, over a notebook. The former chair of the Lacoste School of the Arts, Nancy Herstand, has served on the SCAD Board of Trustees for many years now, ensuring continuity, helping the university remain a good steward of the gift.

Lacoste recreated something we'd lost, the intimacy, the smallness of what SCAD had been in its first days, classes *en plein air*, everybody eating and living and studying together, while also providing students a chance to learn the lessons afforded by travel.

This experience taught me about more than light and color. We learned what it took to open a new campus, to take the SCAD magic and grow it in a new place. Soon, we were announcing plans to open another location in Atlanta, home to many companies and organizations that hired our students, from CNN to Cartoon Network. SCAD Atlanta now enrolls more than two thousand students. And in the years after SCAD Atlanta, we announced the opening of a location in Asia, SCAD Hong Kong, a campus that started with a hundred and now hosts nearly a thousand students.

Each SCAD location has its own character, from the speed and movement of Atlanta, one of the world's great cities for young entrepreneurs, to the international dynamism of Hong Kong, the creative capital of the Far East, to the light and color of Lacoste, a fortress and refuge for many of the world's great artists.

I wish my father had been alive to see it all happen. I want him to know we are doing it, and doing it right.

"As long as it's for the students," he still says, in my heart.

And I know: He would approve.

Chapter Thirteen

Lanterns

"I just got a strange call," my assistant said, one day back in 1991. "Something about a building being demolished. The caller wanted you to know."

This wasn't uncommon. I'd gotten some unusual calls and letters over the years, from community members concerned about suspicious students outside their homes.

"What are the students doing?" I'd ask.

"They have cameras."

And I'd have to apologize and break the bad news to them, that maybe the students were engaged in illicit acts of architectural photography. Sometimes, it'd be parents calling about their children.

"I'm just worried," they'd say. "She doesn't seem to have any direction."

"What year is she?" I'd ask. "Has she picked a major yet?"

"She's seven."

We've gotten more oddball calls about one subject than any other: real estate. Some days, it seemed like everyone on the Eastern Seaboard with or without a real estate license was trying to get us to buy some historic property where General Sherman's troops had bivouacked. According to tour guides and real estate agents and homeowners, Sherman's men commandeered nearly every home in Savannah for some purpose.

"This home was a Union hospital," they'd say.

"Sherman's troops appropriated this one for a saloon."

"His chickens roosted in this very carriage house."

Sometimes the stories were about the Marquis de Lafayette or maybe John and Charles Wesley, but there was always a story. Always.

I suppose it's normal for people to want some connection to a city's myths, but I've fielded too many crazy calls to believe them all, especially calls about buildings, famous people who lived there, slept there.

"What building were they talking about?" I asked.

"The man said something about a depot," she said. "Something about some developer who was going to bust it up and sell off all the Savannah gray bricks for one dollar apiece."

This was the Central of Georgia Railroad Depot, the oldest existing railroad complex in the nation, the beginning and ending of every rail line in America. I decided to go see for myself. Were they really going to raze it?

In the car, across the cobbles of Taylor and Jones Streets, I thought about the sad situation of this property, arguably the most important historic structure in a city full of them. Here was a building where Sherman did more than sleep, as its capture represented the beginning of the end of the rebellion, despite the Confederate soldiers' setting fire to the depot, not wanting the Union to get their hands on a year's worth of cotton, bales of it stacked to the sky—although other stories suggested it was the Union soldiers who burned the depot as a warning to Confederate ships in the river. The one common thread in both versions is that the fire was so bright that it was visible for miles out at sea. Some even said they saw it from Bermuda.

Nearly one hundred years before Sherman, one of the bloodiest battles of the Revolutionary War took place on that same ground. If any earth was sacred in the city, this was it.

By 1991, the property's value was in the much-coveted Savannah gray bricks, fired at Henry McAlpin's Hermitage Plantation upriver. By the late twentieth century, most of the original antebellum depot—the size of two city blocks—had lost its roof. It was less a historic property than a historic *wall*. But some wall.

I was worried we'd get there and find it gone, nothing there but a wrecking ball in the dirt. I hadn't thought my life would turn out like this. I'd read my Jane Jacobs, seen firsthand how cities shape the human imagination, how cities are in many ways the greatest of all human creations, the ultimate act of art and design. The university tried to be a good steward through adaptive reuse projects that respect and retain a building's heritage significance while adding a modern stratum.

For SCAD, education is that modern stratum, the new idea we put into old buildings, just as Jacobs so famously advocated. Across the colonial city of Savannah, the university added new chapters to the stories of its places, and I wondered if we would ever play a role in the story of this depot.

When our car emerged from the trees and turned toward the vast site, though, we saw no flames, no wrecking ball, not a soldier nor an army of hard hats. Just pigeons, and weeds, and the charred walls of the old sheds, hanging on for dear life.

"Maybe it was a prank call," I said.

...

But it was no prank. I made a few inquiries, got the whole story—about the developer who'd bought an option on the property so he could erect a parking garage. A city needs those, but not on hallowed ground. The actual demolition, I was told, was scheduled for four days later. The destruction of the depot threatened to nullify the National Historic Landmark status of the property, risking a domino effect, where Savannah could lose whole swaths of history, whole districts.

A few calls stopped the wrecking ball, but only for a moment.

We needed this property. I just didn't know what we would put there.

"We need dorms," my colleagues in administration said.

"We need an athletics facility," said others.

Athletics played an important role at SCAD, and yet, what this particular site needed was not tennis courts and bleachers.

Every few months, the property tiptoed up the scaffolding to the hangman's noose. Injunctions would stop it, then lapse, then more injunctions. SCAD offered to buy the property, with the promise that we'd preserve what was left of it, and the *Savannah Morning News* announced its support of our efforts: "Clearly," the editorial board wrote, "the SCAD sale is the best of all possible worlds."

We prayed, we hoped, and then, with a chorus of defenders across the city, our lower bid was accepted.

Immediately, we did what work we could to stop the deterioration, braced precipitous walls, fenced off the most perilous areas. To get a sense of the immense size of the property, imagine a parcel of land deep enough to hold the Metropolitan Museum of Art or the Louvre. At one end was what they called the old Gray Building, in the Palladian style, six immense Doric columns holding the pediment. We rechristened it Kiah Hall, in honor of educator, artist, civil rights activist, and SCAD trustee Virginia Kiah, and we set about our work. As always, students were brought in to study the restoration process, how to conserve interior ceilings, how to peel back each layer of paint to expose the same bitumen black used to paint the locomotives. Soon, Kiah Hall would house the Earle W. Newton Collection of British American Art and the Shirrel B. Rhoades Collection, donated to the university.

But behind Kiah Hall, where the holy ground was located, we had no idea what to do with that, its forest of wild indigo and broomweed and brick, those titanic Romanesque arches stretching for two city blocks, where trains had once spilled their secrets and where students now sat on the sidewalk staring through at a safe distance, painting, photographing, drawing, capturing the light through the ruins.

We fenced it off, secured it, set ourselves to dreaming about what it could be. Students sketched a thousand sunsets through its empty arches, and a thousand more, generation after generation of ragweed beaten back, and pretty soon, the university had grown up around it, vast new residence halls on one side, the Ex Libris bookstore on another, Eichberg Hall and the SCAD School of Building Arts to the south, Crites Hall and Bergen Hall to the north, where students studied performing arts and photography.

"I think it's time to do something with the old sheds," I said to Glenn one day in 2007.

"Like what?" he said. "They're so long, the space is endless."

As were the possibilities.

...

We never set out to become one of the world's leading nonprofits devoted to historic preservation and adaptive reuse. In 1979, we bought the Armory because we didn't have the money to build something new. But it was beautiful, and it had a history, and we felt like our tiny little school might benefit from living in a place with a good story.

That's how it started.

That's it.

No grand scheme.

In the years since, the story of the Armory was joined by more stories, of the nunnery where the sisters who taught Justice Clarence Thomas lived, of the Harmonie Social Club, and a power station, a textiles factory, a public health office, and many private homes and nineteenth-century schoolhouses where SCAD students now take classes year-round. In Atlanta, digital media students study in a former NBC affiliate studio and writing students sit with Colson Whitehead and Margaret Atwood and Augusten Burroughs in Ivy Hall, the oldest Queen Anne-style private residence in the Southeastern United States, now a SCAD writing center.

The university thrived in many structures that had originally served altogether different purposes. In Lacoste, we have the boulangerie, where the village's bread was baked for three centuries. A historic synagogue in Savannah is now the student center, a vaudeville playhouse is now home to the Savannah Film Festival, Savannah's first department store is now the Jen Library, where students spend their days, and then go home at night to a redesigned midcentury Howard Johnson motel that's now just one of many SCAD residence halls around the world.

We'd done it all, but we'd never done anything quite like this ancient railroad depot. It was a ruin.

"What should we make here?" Glenn asked, walking the site with me.

"How about a museum?" I said.

...

At about the same time Glenn and I had begun to conceive of a new museum on the site, a SCAD-magic miracle happened. It came in the form of a man named Dr. Walter Evans, a Savannah native who'd become a prominent surgeon in Detroit and one of the world's foremost collectors of African American artwork, representing more than one hundred fifty years of art history. Walter and his wife, Linda, were friends and confidants to many great artists and writers, from Romare Bearden to Alice Walker.

Walter and Linda had returned to Savannah, and they'd quickly become community leaders, investing in the life of the former West Broad Street corridor where the defunct Central of Georgia railroad complex stood. We sat in my office, and he shared his vision.

"We need a home for the art," Walter said.

He wanted somebody who'd take care of it, who wouldn't store it away, a place where schoolchildren and students could benefit from hearing and seeing and learning the tales the art could tell. I took Walter to the site, where the walls were all that stood of the old depot.

"What if the work lived here?" I said. "The Walter O. Evans Collection of African American Art at the new SCAD Museum of Art."

He looked long and hard at the ground and then looked up and told me a story.

Two slaves from a plantation near Macon, he said, once came to this depot. This was long before the Emancipation Proclamation. But they'd heard about the Declaration of Independence, and they'd made up their minds to seek out a new life and liberty, the pursuit of their own happiness.

"Their names were William and Ellen Craft," he said. "And they devised a plan. A plan to escape."

Ellen, fair skinned, would pose as a wealthy white planter, a man, and William would be her valet. Together they would come to Savannah, then board the train heading north to free states.

On a winter morning in 1848, Ellen donned homemade pants and green glasses and covered her newly shorn hair with a top hat. She wrapped her arm in a sling to avoid having to sign her name, and to dissuade conversation, she feigned deafness.

"They boarded the Macon train, she in first class, William in the slave car," he said, "and they arrived right here, right where the platform used to be."

The Crafts then switched trains and headed north, transcending race, class, even gender on their way to freedom.

Walter and I sat down with Bob Jepson, another benevolent, kindhearted, generous university donor, and launched a capital development campaign.

We broke ground on a rainy, cold January afternoon in 2010.

"I wish it were a prettier day," I said to Walter.

"The rain is just making the ground soft," he said. "So we can get to work."

...

I had only one person in mind to design the new museum: Christian Sottile. He ran an urban design firm in Savannah with his wife, Amy, whom he met while they were students at SCAD. Christian had created the most important city plans for Savannah since General Oglethorpe conceived of the squares, and he was known around the nation and the world for his passion, his intelligence, and his belief that design should be mindful of history but not enslaved to it. Best of all, he was valedictorian of the SCAD Class of 1997, and earned a Master of Architecture from SCAD.

In 2011, I named him dean of the SCAD School of Building Arts.

Christian and I walked the site, talking, while he sketched ideas.

I shared my thoughts with him, how we needed a gallery dedicated to alumni artists, and a gallery dedicated to the Evans Collection and African American artists, an experiential gallery, a theater for lectures, a café, studio spaces for the Collaborative Learning Center, a courtyard and outdoor theater, and, of course, classrooms, where students from across disciplines could take advantage of the closeness of the exhibitions.

"The question," Christian said, touching the ruins with his hand, "is what can all this be? It's not a depot anymore."

"And it doesn't need to be."

"But these walls, these bricks."

"Seventy thousand bricks," I said. "At last count. And I want to use all of them."

We wanted to do more than build a museum around a few old walls. We wanted to do something civic, something monumental.

What he envisioned was a dialogue of contrasts, where a new concrete structure would rise inside the original perimeter of the historic brick ruins. Where walls were gone or crumbling, smooth concrete surfaces would emerge.

"We're building a structure that will be a part of the cityscape forever," he said. "Original materials, new execution. Endings, beginnings."

We would preserve the ruins as we found them—and start from scratch. A new building with a storied history. The SCAD Museum of Art would become a conversation between past and present.

It took nearly two years. Hard hats were all the rage in those days, when my hair remained in the shape of a construction helmet for weeks at a time. In the tradition of Frank Lloyd Wright, I wanted to cohere the entire design into a single mise-en-scène, from the walls to the stairs to the hardware on the doors. I wanted *everything* to be designed, considered, thought about.

The SCAD team, led by Glenn and me, consisted of dozens of dedicated staff who stayed busy with the project on winged feet. Christian designed and realized our classrooms, a student lounge, a terrace overlooking a courtyard, the entire space a cathedral of learning, with whiteboards and computer labs and a herculean digital tablet that we designed ourselves. At twelve feet long, it was—at the time—the largest interactive device in the world, at least the largest intended for use by the public, designed for guests to learn more about the museum's exhibitions and collections.

As historic preservationists say, "The greenest building is the one that's already built," but we went even further, by using renewable materials and energy-efficient structural elements, outfitting the museum with low-energy light fixtures, zoned climate control, exterior cooling towers, low-flow plumbing fixtures, and low-emissivity glass. Scattered excess bricks were incorporated into the park-like Alex Townsend Memorial Courtyard, and reclaimed heart pine timber trusses were transformed into acoustical slat walls for the museum theater, surrounding the audience in a cocoon.

It wasn't just the building that'd be innovative; the programming would be equally unorthodox, especially for an academic museum. We would not try to build huge collections and then raise money just to store the art, keeping it locked away. I listened to my wise and wonderful friend Lorlee Tenenbaum, who advised that we create a mutable space, revolving, fluid, something new every season. The SCAD museum would be open to artists from other countries, with new exhibitions every time visitors returned. It wouldn't be one museum—it'd be a thousand museums.

"If this place is a dialogue," I said to Christian, "we need a climax."

"The high point," he said.

"A statement."

"I have some ideas."

What we needed was a signature structural feature, a memorable architectural element that would be, in and of itself, a work of art. We talked and talked, about the history of the place, what it meant then, what it meant now. We discussed the great fires of 1864, the place as a point of departure for newly freed slaves on Emancipation Day.

"It's a phoenix," Christian said. "This structure burns, collapses, is wracked by war and time, and now it has risen, high."

What he conceived of, in the end, was brilliant—literally.

It was perfect, an eighty-six-foot-tall tower of light, a beacon of balefire to draw visitors from around the world, prismatic, reflecting, absorptive, capturing sunlight during the day and providing a diffuse glow in the evening, marking the entrance to more than eighty thousand new square feet of museum space.

He showed me the sketch.

"I'm calling it a lantern," he said. "Translucent glass and steel. A tower of light."

…

On opening night, in the fall of 2011, we anticipated a few hundred students, and when we arrived, I was shocked to see lines snaking out both sides of the building, right under the gleaming white lantern.

"How many students are here?" I asked Glenn.

"They stopped counting at twenty-five hundred," he said.

Inside, the students laughed, smiled, picked their jaws up from the floor, absorbing everything from the work; sculptures and reliefs by Liza Lou; portraits by Kehinde Wiley; a SCAD-commissioned video installation by Bill Viola; another site-specific sculptural installation by Kendall Buster; and selections from the Walter O. Evans Collection of African American Art by Jacob Lawrence, Aaron Douglas, and nearly forty more artists. All night, I overheard bits of jubilant conversation among the students, who couldn't believe we'd made this for them.

I was swept away in a surge of joyful tears, my hand grabbed by faculty friends who wanted to show me a favorite piece, my arms enveloping Walter, and plenty of high fives from members of the university's Design Group team, who'd dedicated two years to this sublime work of art and architecture.

The SCAD Museum of Art would go on to be featured on CNN, in magazines and newspapers, the critics swooning, the public raving, the students gasping, and the building receiving accolade after accolade, including the American Institute of Architects' National Honor Award for Architecture. Christian, too, was honored with the AIA Young Architects Award. In the four years since it opened, tens of thousands of visitors have rejoiced in their experience on this sacred ground. The whole precinct around the museum has seen new life. What was once a ruined plat of careworn desolation is now full of life, students walking to class, back to their rooms, to dream dreams born in these old walls that long ago we raced to rescue.

I still think of the Crafts, their powerfully courageous, creative act of freedom. And I think of the enormous hearts and visions of Savannahians like Walter and Linda and Bob and Alice Jepson and many, many others over the years who have helped make it possible for Savannah to sail proudly into another century by preserving the best of its past, and pushing on toward an even more remarkable future.

Not long ago, Glenn, Madison, and I were in the car on our way to an exhibition of Oscar de la Renta's work in the André Leon Talley Gallery, the museum's lantern shining brightly across the city skyline, and I had to laugh.

To think, someone had wanted to make it a parking garage.

Chapter Fourteen

Honey

A few years ago, a certain kind of unexpected visitor began showing up at my office at Lai Wa Hall, a former residence on Forsyth Park where we installed the executive administration offices about ten years ago. We have always gotten drop-in callers at Lai Wa, the usual stray tourists looking for a trolley stop, the brides who frequently pose on our front steps. But these particular visitors were not usual, and they had one thing in common: They were college presidents. Sometimes, they would call or write first; sometimes they would just show up at the front door.

"There's someone here to see you," my assistant would say.

"Who?"

"He's the president of _____ University."

"Really?" I would say. "Here?"

"In the lobby."

The first few times this happened, I panicked for a second. Had I forgotten an appointment? An accreditation visit?

Soon, this fellow president and I would be seated in a cozy, paneled alcove where I prefer to hold meetings—somewhere between a parlor and a study, stacked to the ceiling with books. We would chat about their work, and they would explain that they were preparing to write a strategic plan or were new to the job and looking for ideas. And then they would reveal the true reason they had come. They wanted to know the secret. Most didn't come right out and ask. But some did.

"The secret?" I'd ask, laughing.

A decade ago, a few years after I'd been named president of SCAD, we began earning some pretty impressive awards from

Newsweek, Forbes, U.S. News & World Report, DesignIntelligence, 3D World, Huffington Post, and others: "America's Best Colleges," "America's Best Graduate Schools," "America's Best Colleges for Entrepreneurs," "Hottest for Studying Art," and top rankings for interior design, industrial design, animation, fashion, and more. University presidents might pretend these accolades don't really matter, but the external validation of one's lifetime of labors is no small thing.

These presidents who visit, I suppose they've heard from colleagues about the SCAD secret sauce or have been urged by their boards to find the magic elixir, and then they come to see for themselves. Some want to know how we plan or conduct our fundraising, while others want to know how I've structured my office staff. I sat with one president who asked to see the organizational chart. He studied it like it held secrets to the location of buried treasure.

On a few of these early visits by college presidents, some of them even called me names. Well, sort of. "What's your biggest challenge as a CEO?" they asked.

CEO.

Nobody had ever called me that before. CEOs operated global companies, managed budgets larger than the gross domestic product of small nations, rang bells on the New York Stock Exchange. That's what a CEO was—not a tiny little teacher in regalia, presiding over the turning of tassels in a small Southern town. I'd just never thought of myself in those terms. It's hard to fuss too much over titles when, in the same week, you've written the catalog and cleaned the toilets.

Regardless of titles—CEO, college president, you name it—it's no surprise that many of these visiting administrators are looking for answers. Higher education is in crisis, they remind me, citing this or that statistic from the latest report or op-ed about the precipitous state of higher learning: enrollments shrinking, debt ballooning, the race to keep the doors open.

At SCAD, we've grown enrollment every year since I became president—from 4,923 students in 2000 to 12,456 in 2015—and these presidents want to know how.

If there's a secret to SCAD's success, it's in asking a single question: How are we different? In other words, what are the distinctive, substantive qualities that set our university apart in higher education? College is the most important financial decision in an individual's and a family's life—next to buying a home—and the choice will influence the rest of one's life. A college president must be able to sit across the table from a prospective family and explain, clearly, why that institution is the right institution. From the very beginning, SCAD set itself apart from other universities in four unique ways:

First, no large lecture classes. None.

Second, all classes taught by credentialed faculty.

Third, no Friday classes, so students and faculty have time for individualized teaching and learning.

Fourth, a mission unapologetically focused on professional career preparation, without sacrificing the liberal arts and humanities.

These qualities are in SCAD's DNA. They are who we are. When I became president, that didn't change. But I knew we needed to go further to stay competitive in the twenty-first century.

...

One of SCAD's greatest strengths, the milieu in which all of our successes are born, is our ability to effect change in sudden, inspired bursts. We can turn on a dime.

Intransigence is one major challenge at older, established universities, where an institution can be too sclerotic to innovate, too slow to respond to unanticipated conditions. For some college presidents, the biggest challenge is in getting the right people in the room to address the challenge. I've heard the stories, how tenured faculty members don't always respond to emails, how one chair is notoriously churlish, another always on the road, how deans and vice presidents have their own fiefdoms to worry about. The president's problem is just that: the president's problem, not theirs.

What a nightmare.

Even if you can get all the right people in the room, there's still no guarantee you can get anything accomplished. Committees must be formed. Subcommittees. Working groups. A new email address for the work group must be obtained. Surveys must be deployed, websites launched for the gathering of feedback on the name of the work group, on which the subcommittee must vote before passing it on to the committee for consideration.

There's nothing inherently wrong with thoughtful, measured deliberation about a serious matter, but deliberation for its own sake stymies innovation. At SCAD, we move fast. We harbor no fiefdoms.

Because of this ability to act and react with speed and agility, we can create new initiatives and change course in head-spinning time.

I can remember a hot August day in 2009, as our SCAD team prepared for a preliminary visit from SACSCOC, in advance of the following year's visit to reaffirm the institution's accreditation. In this preparatory visit, a few faculty and administrators were scheduled to present an early draft of the university's Quality Enhancement Plan (QEP), inviting feedback from the SACSCOC representatives. Focus groups had been convened, research had been gathered. As the meeting neared, I reviewed the work group's initial plan and found that it was missing something. In short, the plan—a proposed initiative focused on teaching students how to collaborate with local governments on public art projects—just didn't feel like us. There was little in the plan addressing the SCAD mission and our mandate to prepare students for careers. Sure, some graduates would go on to work with communities on public art projects, but not most.

A day before the scheduled presentation of the plan, I called in members of the work group and other key staff.

"Let's think bigger," I said. "Why limit these collaborations to local municipalities or small art installations? How about we teach students how to collaborate with many different kinds of external partners?"

"Like who?" one faculty member asked.

"Why not companies?" I asked. "Why not major brands? Why not big firms like the ones that hire our graduates?"

Our students were going on to careers in industrial design, advertising, film, jewelry, design management, I reasoned. Shouldn't we be preparing those students to collaborate, too?

"What would our students collaborate with them on?" someone asked.

"We could invite the external partner to present a design challenge," one dean suggested. "Like we do in industrial design."

"Exactly," I said.

In less than an hour, we developed a relevant Quality Enhancement Plan for the university, including a blueprint for a Collaborative Learning Center where all manner of external partners—from nonprofits to multinational corporations to local businesses—could present funded design challenges. In these projects, SCAD students would create real solutions: brand realignments, reimagined retail interiors, new adverts, social media campaigns, you name it.

Less than a year later, the SCAD Collaborative Learning Center, or CLC, would open at all university locations. Since 2010, its first year of operation, the CLC has hosted approximately 180 projects for 2,533 students, 130 faculty, and 113 external partners, including Google, Apple, BMW, General Electric, Coca-Cola, and FOX Sports, to name only a very few—with these partners contributing funds that support scholarships, prizes, student travel, and more. While some universities teach entrepreneurship through the incubation of startups, which understandably have a high failure rate, SCAD partners students with established companies. Students contribute ideas and tangible solutions to brands that desire fresh thinking. Deadline-driven, results-oriented CLC experiences challenge students and prepare them for their own careers. Not infrequently, those experiences lead to internships and job offers for students and graduates. I like to think that optimal synergies occur at SCAD because we are nimble. We can put egos aside and create mission-focused action plans in a timely manner. Most universities can't do that.

...

This ability to ruminate, then change and adapt quickly, has always been a part of the university's character. I still remember, clear as day, the moment in 1985 when students started asking about computers.

"Computers?" I remember asking. "For art students?"

Back then, computers were for actuaries and rocket launches, not creative careers, at least not in higher education. I asked around. We had just hired a polymath named Jim Alley to teach painting, photography, and math. He had an interesting academic background and could teach a number of subjects. He had been toying with the idea of manipulating images and making art with personal computers. A few students also had begun slogging their heavy desktop setups into the dorm, and a few of these students started telling us about a new machine they had read about, a computer created specifically for artists, with color graphics and great sound.

"It's called the Amiga," Jim explained.

"Can we teach with it?" I asked.

"Maybe," he said. "I think we should give this computer thing a try."

Before they went on sale, we called Commodore and ordered the first twenty-five they could ship; pretty soon, we had two or three computer art courses on the books. Then Jim turned his attention to Apple and became quite an expert, eventually writing a regular column for *Macworld*. While other art departments and schools were dragging their paintbrushes and their heels, we were early adopters of new technologies in art and design. Historic methods were and remain vital, but we wanted our students to express multitudes of meanings, as they wished.

Within a decade of our initial experiments with computers, we were offering one of the first degree programs in computer art in the world and would go on to create the first Bachelor of Fine Arts and Master of Fine Arts programs in motion media design, visual effects, game development, and more. Today, over 1,000 SCAD students major in animation alone.

Back in 1995, two of our earliest computer art majors, Jeremy Roush and Steve LaVietes, approached us with an idea. They had been learning how to use 360-degree cameras in their classes, and they wanted to transform the SCAD admission catalog into a digital artifact. They gathered a group of classmates—they were students, mind you—and we provided them with 360-degree cameras and sent them on their way. They called their team Satellite, which was appropriate, seeing as they circled around the SCAD universe, touring buildings, watching, observing, capturing images and scenes, creating sound effects, working all night, and sleeping on the floors of their editing suites. They ran wild with the project, and when we presented the finished product—CDs, and later, DVDs—to prospective students at college fairs, these stunning virtual "catalogs" were an instant hit. People couldn't believe these discs were free, created mostly by students.

Needless to say, I was not surprised in the least when, in 2013, Steve won an Academy Award for technical achievement. I like to think that he won that award, in part, because we set him loose with early computer art technology when he was still a student. We couldn't have known what he would make, but we knew he had a prodigious intellect, and we had the technology.

In both these instances, 1985 and 1995, did we know what students would do with these technologies? No. Did any of us know that these machines and their successors would transform everything we knew of art and design education? No. Did we know that it would be years after our first experiments with Satellite before other universities would begin putting their catalogs online, in digital form? No. All these innovations and experiments, which look quite prescient now, were simply the result of doing what we've always endeavored to do at SCAD: We listened to the students, who are often strikingly in tune with the vibrations of tomorrow—signals the rest of us are not calibrated to hear.

...

When I became president, I wanted to keep alive this same spirit of openness to new ideas across the curriculum. If someone could make a good argument that a degree program needed to change, I wanted to champion that change. And change we did. In 2000, the university offered fifty-five programs of study in eighteen disciplines. Today, SCAD offers ninety-nine programs in forty-four disciplines—several of those degree programs the first of their kind in higher education, such as the Master of Fine Arts in themed entertainment design, born out of a conversation I had with one of Disney's leading Imagineers, or the new Bachelor of Fine Arts degree program in user experience (UX) design that SCAD recently created in collaboration with Google. In this new cobranded degree program, students learn to tackle complex digital challenges in health care technology, automotive interior design, mobile phone systems, and more. Dean of the SCAD School of Design Victor Ermoli and other faculty and staff leaders, including John Paul Rowan and Josh Lind at the CLC, were key in the launching of this new program.

We've created many programs just like this one within a single academic year, which, in higher education, is rare. Like a writer working feverishly through the night to finish an inspired new novel, we work fast to get our best ideas on the page.

And yet, like that novelist, we can't be afraid to kill our

proverbial darlings, either. As president, I have invented as well as retired programs of study—which is unheard of at many institutions. In 1979, for example, we offered a degree in ceramics, but as academic dean, I quickly realized that graduates would have great difficulty making a living at throwing pots. So we discontinued it. These are never easy decisions, but they keep SCAD competitive, responsive, fresh, new. In addition to the forty-four programs of study we've added since 2000, I have also led the elimination of nineteen faltering programs.

Those were tough, but necessary, decisions.

Necessary, because when we eliminate programs with little demand, the university can then invest those resources in powerful, mission-focused new initiatives. In 2013, Dean Christian Sottile launched SCADpad, where students and faculty from twelve departments worked to address the challenge of housing in the world's great cities. The students' elegant solution was not only designed but actually built: a ground-breaking micro-housing community set within an existing, underutilized midcentury urban parking deck. The project, created by seventy-five students, thirty-seven alumni, and twelve faculty members, debuted in 2014, giving students exposure to real-world conditions and practical experiences in solving immediate needs in their communities. Since its launch, twenty-eight students, faculty members, and journalists have been housed at SCADpad—on the fourth level of the SCAD Atlanta parking structure—and the project has been covered by the *Today* show, *TIME*, CNN, *Architectural Record*, and others. In 2014, SCADpad earned the World Architecture News Urban Design Award.

Just a few months ago, we opened SCAD FASH, a new museum of fashion and film that exists at the international intersection of study, exhibition, and discourse. We also just launched the SCAD Alumni Atelier, where the university provides a creative residency for our alumni, inviting graduates back to campus locations across the world to create new work and share their discoveries, processes, and ideas with the college community. We couldn't create initiatives like these if the institution were saddled with foundering academic departments, empty classrooms, unwanted degree programs, or outsized athletics programs.

Speaking of athletics—sometimes our guests don't get it.

"Sports at an art school?" more than one visiting administrator has said.

"The students asked for it," I explain.

That's another essential ingredient to SCAD: We try to listen to our students, even when what they're saying sounds impossible or strange, or both.

In 1984, a few students asked for a soccer team.

"Sure," we said.

It would be a club team, an experiment. English professor Lew Tate would coach.

Then students asked for lacrosse, then golf, swimming, rowing, tennis, baseball, softball, basketball, and volleyball. In time, we hired full-time coaches, joined a conference, and made a go of it. Why not? Nobody told our art students they weren't supposed

to love sports. And it's no secret that competitive athletic teams helped broaden the university's appeal. We had something many arts universities didn't. Another distinguishing factor.

Better still, these student-artist-athletes have what we look for in all young creative professionals: discipline, heart, character, and the ability to shake off a rejection or a loss and continue to strive. In the late nineties, one of our students from Ecuador wrote me a letter asking where she could board her horse during the academic year, which led to a conversation with her and other students who competed in equitation. A decade later, after a significant donation by benefactor Ron Waranch, we launched a new Bachelor of Arts in equestrian studies and opened the SCAD Ronald C. Waranch Equestrian Center, now home to one of the most-lauded equestrian programs in the nation, earning more than two dozen team and individual national titles and honors.

Nevertheless, I have had to retire some athletics programs over the years, when I felt those resources would serve students better elsewhere, and that has not been an easy thing to do. But we have honored scholarships, and most of those students have stayed with us to complete their degree programs, which is why they came here in the first place.

At some point during my tours with guests, the conversation always turns to one unmistakable fact: Art is everywhere, in meeting rooms, classrooms, even restrooms.

"This must be a gallery," they say, of this or that random hallway.

"No, the gallery's just up ahead."

This level of art saturation is rare, I think, even for an art and design university. It's not just because we love beauty, I explain to guests. The intentional placement of thousands of works of art in direct proximity to students is a strategic decision, another distinguishing factor of SCAD. Students are immersed in art and observe quality, just by walking around every SCAD campus.

Our mission is to prepare students for professional careers, and one way we do that is by purchasing a great deal of student and alumni art every year. Students benefit tremendously from this process, learning how to price their work, how to prepare it for sale, transport it, deliver it. And when they see it on display somewhere around the university, the pride on their faces is unmistakable.

At last count, the SCAD Permanent Collection included 11,376 works of art created by literally thousands of students, faculty, and alumni; as I write this, nearly six thousand of those works are hanging somewhere at SCAD facilities in Savannah, Atlanta, Lacoste, or Hong Kong. This number doesn't include the collections at the SCAD Museum of Art—an estimated five thousand pieces—or work in the dozens of university galleries on three continents, where, in the past academic year, we hosted more than sixty exhibitions.

These days, when visitors assume this or that hallway is a gallery, I don't disabuse them.

They're right. It is.

...

All our distinctive qualities—our speed, our innovative degree programs, our unique initiatives such as the Collaborative Learning

Center—clearly help SCAD distinguish itself in the crowded field of higher education, but there's one final ingredient to the secret sauce: people. People like Danny Filson and Christina Routhier, who helped build the Savannah Film Festival into the most delightful, friendliest festival at any university in the nation; and Kari Herrin and Laurie Ann Farrell, who helped put SCAD deFINE ART on the map; and Walter Evans and Bob Jepson, who helped make the SCAD Museum of Art a reality; and André Leon Talley, who helped make the SCAD Fashion Show the most-watched fashion show in higher education. Every university president needs an André—this dear friend and native son of the South, who studied French at Brown University, worked with Warhol at *Interview*, found his way into the graces of Diana Vreeland, and served as an editor, among other roles, for *Vogue*. He is a writer, raconteur, stylist, muse, sage, wit, critic, historian, and, to many, the ultimate voice of authority on all matters of style and culture.

At a recent Art of the Mind lecture, hosted by the SCAD School of Liberal Arts, the speaker—a writer for Cartoon Network's *Adventure Time*—spoke about collaboration.

"Find people you like and work with them," he said. "It's that simple. If you're lucky, you'll find people who love all the strange, weird, funny things you love, and if you do, you should make something together."

I was lucky enough to find people like André.

We invited him to be honored with a Lifetime Achievement Award back in 2001, at our fledgling SCAD Fashion Show, and when he arrived, Danny, master host and tour guide, showed him around the Savannah campus, the historic buildings scattered across the city like wildflowers. They visited the Jen Library first, even though André protested.

"Mr. Filson," he said. "I love books, but I have no interest in this library."

But Danny insisted, and pretty soon André was admiring how we had taken an old downtown department store and redesigned it to evoke a luxury liner of the early twentieth century, and how we had transformed a nineteenth-century dry goods store into Ex Libris, the SCAD Savannah bookstore, disguising its ironwork pillars with tessellated stacks of old legal books, volumes and volumes spiraling to the ceiling like cave formations of the literary gods.

"Who did this?" André exclaimed. "I must meet this person right now!"

Danny brought André over to my office, and we became fast friends, sharing a love for classics and for the nouveau, for the finest detail in design, and for the subtext in every story, the meaning proffered in every aesthetic choice, down to every ruffle, every line, and the beveled edges of every table. He served on the Board of Trustees for thirteen years, and he champions SCAD among the great artists and designers of our age, bringing talents like Miuccia Prada, Zac Posen, Tom Ford, Vera Wang, Marc Jacobs, Diane von Furstenberg, Manolo Blahnik, and others to the university.

That's why I say every college president needs an André, an angel, a champion, a friend. And we have many of those. We've got an Albie (Whitaker), an Anita (Thomas), a Bob (Nardelli), a (Chan) Lai Wa, a Nancy (Herstand), a P.J. (Johnson), a Sally (Waranch Rajcic), a Stuart (Saunders), and others: trustees, donors, and secret weapons who help move the mission forward in ways only they can.

In my decade and a half as president of SCAD, I am fortunate to have found people who love what I love, and we have made some significant strides together.

We've come so far.

SCAD has four physical locations on three continents (plus online), and is an institution with 1,886 faculty and staff and 109 facilities around the world, more than triple the square footage we had when I took the reins. I can remember discussing the possibility of our creating an endowment back in 2000, to fund scholarships. We started with nothing, and with the help of major donors and board volunteers who believe in our work, we grew it to $55 million last year, $83 million this year. The SCAD Endowment goal for 2018 is $175 million, all to support and sustain exceptional student learning.

Wow.

Wow wow wow.

We've grown so much, in so many ways. You bet I'm proud of our extraordinary SCAD team, our work ethic. I am especially proud of the character and work of our students.

When I moved to Savannah, I was a schoolteacher. Young, full of hope. Now, nearly forty years later, when I consider how expansive, complex, and multifaceted the university has become, I suppose a CEO-educator is exactly what I am.

These days, we have as many corporate executives touring the university as we do college presidents. Just the other day, I found myself showing Georgia Governor Nathan Deal around campus, and we ran into another set of visitors at Kiah Hall, home to the Collaborative Learning Center. These guests were executives with Home Depot and Google, here to work with students on different collaborative projects. When I first became president, I might've been astounded that such a moment could be possible at SCAD, these persons representing business, government, technology, and some of the most creative thinking in human history.

"We're just here to learn," one of the Google executives said.

"Isn't that what college is for?" Governor Deal said.

I couldn't have said it better myself.

Chapter Fifteen

Sisters

I have lived amid a great whirling frenzy of joy and work and people, and at the great center of this firmament is a person whose very existence on this earth made me whole. Her name is Pam, and she is my sister, and the world wasn't right until she came into it.

"Please, Mommy," I said when I was four years old. "Please. Judy has a little sister. Catherine has a little sister. Margaret has *two* little sisters. Two!"

"Don't be silly, Paula," Mom said.

"Pleeeeeeeeeease."

"Maybe," Mom said. "If you pray about it, and wish upon every star."

I wished *hard*, on stars, on lucky pennies tucked into the pockets of my skirts, on the downy fluff I blew from seeding dandelions while sitting on the stoop.

"Make sure it's a girl," I said, as the dandelion seeds took flight on a hot summer wind.

Then one cool fall day, wood smoke filling the air, my mother and father looked at me across the dinner table and told me.

"We're going to have a baby," Mom said.

"Really?" I said. "I mean, really?"

"Really."

"Are you sure?"

"We're pretty sure."

"And you're sure it's a girl?"

My father laughed.

"Well, maybe."

What I really wanted was a little sister, somebody who looked like my doll. The next day, I was surprised to learn that my little sister had not yet arrived, nor the day after, nor the week after. Thanksgiving and Christmas were suitable distractions, but come winter, I was not very pleased with the delay, and by the first day of spring I'd begun to worry.

"Where is she?"

"She's in here," Mom said, pointing to her belly.

But I knew better than that. Babies came from the sky, from heaven, from somewhere, anywhere but bellies. They were found in trees, like peaches, or in baskets, like Easter treasures. I searched, around every corner, under every blooming azalea, looking for something more precious than a golden egg. And then one day, my father called me into the kitchen and told me it was time.

"For what?"

"To go see your sister."

I was shocked. Had she been found? Had the stork come to the house and nobody told me? I put on a freshly pressed dress that my mother had laid out for just this occasion, and we got in the car and drove.

"Why are we at the hospital?"

"This is where they are."

Of course. A hospital. I hadn't thought of that. It was a great place to hide a baby.

Soon, there came my mother and a nurse through the double doors, holding the swaddle of springtime. Mom knelt down to show me, and there she was: my baby, my treasure, my Pam. I fell hopelessly in love.

I reached out to hold her, but they stopped me.

"One day," my mother said. "She's very delicate."

"Oh, I won't hurt the little baby!" I said, the tears already welling. I didn't understand how anyone might think I couldn't be trusted. It was I who willed her into being, after all.

"You'll have your whole life to hold her," my father said.

...

We were *soror mea*, *amica mea*, sisters, friends, reflections, dancing partners, a musical act whose melodies were never ceasing. We were nearly five years apart, but as soon as Pam could walk and talk, that time collapsed to nothing. Before she had come, I was a zero, a nonentity, waiting for the other half of me. Who had I been before Pam? I can't remember. I see photographs of the toddler me, standing by my father's knee under the shade of some Georgia tree, waiting on someone to play with, with bitten lip and squinted eyes, looking up, skyward, waiting.

Even our names sounded alike, the plosive, proud *P*—Pam and Paula, the Poetter girls, a matched pair. We shared a room, each of us with a little twin bed, where we whispered deep into the night, me telling her revised versions of fairy tales, rewriting the story to suit her age, the weather, the season. Sometimes Snow White fled into the forest, sometimes she went trick-or-treating down the street. Usually there were two, Snow White and her sister, Summer White. And always, always, always two Cinderellas, scrubbing the floor, going to the ball, racing home, fitting our feet into two glass slippers, one for each of us. As she got older, she joined in, performed the story I narrated, standing up on her bed, acting out every role in the story, witch or wicked stepmother or the Big Bad Wolf or Prince Charming or the Cowardly Lion, throwing herself onto all fours while I buried my face in the pillow, laughing.

"We're going to get in trouble!" I'd say, coming up for air. We laughed until we cried.

We read books together, too, and Pam was the Emily to my Charlotte, the Laura to my Mary. During the preternaturally long summers on our grandmother's farm, we read aloud all the *Little House on the Prairie* books, and when the books were all finished, we ran outside to re-create the stories ourselves.

Coming home to Atlanta after one summer, we shrieked with delight to see that our father had built us a playhouse in the backyard as a surprise, and we immediately set about keeping house. My early affinity for urban development and interior design was clearly already revealing itself, as we built villages around our new playhouse, raking pine straw into the shapes of rooms, walls, doorways, furnishing these homes with fixtures of our own design, also from straw.

"Where does this chair go?" Pam would say, an armful of straw concealing her face.

"There, near the credenza."

"What's a credenza?"

"I don't know," I'd say.

We would design our rooms, our homes, our playhouse, then redesign them anew every day, and on rainy days, we'd continue designing experiences in cardboard boxes and under card tables, stacking Lincoln Logs, aligning layers of tongue depressors and Elmer's glue to form Swedish cope-style roofs. We built castles, cottages, ski lodges, mud huts, rawhide teepees, through the fall and winter and spring, and then we'd be back in Mississippi for the summer, having graduated from little houses on distant prairies to musical numbers, rehearsing all day for the dinner-and-a-show that night, when our family congregated on the porch.

Pam and I would open the front doors wide, creating a backstage, hanging a sheet for a curtain. "Ladies and gentlemen, the show shall begin in five minutes!" Pam would say, peeking out while the grown-ups sat on the swing, waiting. My Aunt Bess was the lighting director, flashlight in hand.

I'd start the overture.

"Ladies and gentlemen," Pam would say again, this time in a new costume and a new voice, "the show will begin momentarily."

And then, rather dramatically, the music stopped, and a hand extended from the curtain, Pam's little birdlike arm holding a miniature straw hat, no larger than a tea cozy, Pam and I stifling laughter, and I'd launch into "The Mexican Hat Dance" on the piano while my sister danced gaily around the world's tiniest sombrero.

These performances were always varied, always riotously fun, nights of love and laughter and family that linger in my memory as the happiest moments of a happy life, Pam and Paula, Paula and Pam, working hard to delight others, and delighting in the work, whatever that work was, dancing, playing, singing. I deeply enjoyed seeing how my sister could warm to any crowd, no matter how large or small, four adults on a porch, or four hundred in the Briarwood High School auditorium. When I see *The Sound of Music* on television, I don't hear the lovely Julie Andrews. No, I see my sister, twirling and dancing on the stage, telling us about her favorite things.

Even when I entered my teenage years, Pam and I remained close. She joined my gang of buddies, and like Tinkerbell with her fairy dust, she made every moment sweeter, an indispensable member of the ensemble wherever we went, football games, picnics, drive-in movies. On the day I left for college, I hugged her tight.

"Who will play the piano for me?" she said, looking up.

"You have lots of friends," I said.

"But nobody plays like you," she said. "You know all the songs."

She buried her head in my chest, and we hugged awhile longer.

"We'll play songs at Christmas," I said. "We'll fill the house with them."

An hour down the road, on the way to Furman University, I made another wish, a wish that we could play together again one day, someday.

It would be many years before that wish came true, but it did.

Right about the time we were walking through the Armory for the first time, Pam had been out of college for three years, having graduated with her teaching certification and married her college sweetheart, Don. Like my mother and me, Pam had the distinction of studying elementary education and then making the perfectly illogical choice of working in higher education. With her gift for story and language, she worked in communications at the University of Tennessee at Nashville, then the University of South Carolina, following her husband's career advancements with her own, eventually landing at the Southern Baptist Theological Seminary in Louisville, Kentucky, where she wrote and produced university publications.

Throughout the early eighties, we traded ideas. I'd studied every art college catalog written in English and had learned a few things, and Pam had her own ideas about what made a good brochure, pamphlet, catalog. She sent me examples of her work, and I sent her my edits, which she must have found hilarious, because when I sent her copies of our new SCAD catalogs, she did the same, spilling more red ink than I had, but never stingy with the smiley faces and the occasional "Wow!"

"Are you two editing one another's work again?" my father asked over Thanksgivings and Christmases, when we traded work talk about the joys and trials of writing for a university.

And then tragedy struck, when Pam's husband, Don, still in his thirties, was diagnosed with cancer. Their life together had only just begun.

"It wasn't supposed to be like this," she said.

Throughout his illness, Pam soldiered on, and somehow she managed her career and household and the care of her two young children, Kevin and Kimberly, while her husband lay in a bed, dying.

In less than a year, Don was gone.

It wasn't fair for a young mother to go through it alone.

"It's time somebody took care of you," I said. "Come live here."

Our parents were here in Savannah, I reminded her. And her children's symbiotic cousins, Marisa and John Paul. They needed somebody to play with.

"What would I do in Savannah?" she said, through tears.

"I know a little art college," I said. "They need a good writer."

In the blink of an eye, we were together again, two peas in a pod, arm in arm, side by side through the city's squares on the way to offices or meetings or the printer, to pick up proofs of the latest catalog and arm-wrestle over what sounded better, *which* or *that*, scanning for the interpositions of *their* and *they're* and *there* and *to* and *too* and *two* and *it's* and *its*. I had my editorial peeves; she had hers. She fretted about commas, while I had a long list of words that I could not abide, overused adjectives like *wonderful* and *glad* and *creative*.

"We used *thrilled* too much in this part," I'd say, pointing to a page in a proof. "Thrilled, thrilled, everybody's thrilled. What does that even mean, *thrilled*?"

"It's better than *excited*," she'd say. "Maybe we should be *amazed*."

And we'd sit down, figure it out, whatever it was, a catalog, brochure, banner, application form, student handbook. She'd write and I'd edit, I'd write and she'd edit, and it was dizzying and delightful, as though we were children again, rewriting the great fairy tales of our youth.

Marisa and John Paul loved being near their cousins, all of them quite close in age, the four of them like musketeers, running pell-mell through the marshes and forests of our neighborhood, building forts, walking dogs, chasing squirrels. Pam and I watched from the porch and smiled, my hand reaching out for hers, squeezing.

"You're home," I said.

"I know."

In addition to all her work writing and editing catalogs and reports and handbooks, she'd been named as the founding editor of *The Georgia Guardian*, a weekly community newspaper published by SCAD for nearly a decade, earning the Georgia Press Association's highest award for General Excellence.

When our parents retired, Pam took on the task of managing the university's admission office, in addition to her other roles, picking up where our mother left off. My sister had a gift for working with students, especially our PreBees. Like any great speaker, she had mastery of the delicate balance between lightness of heart and seriousness of purpose. She could write sidesplittingly funny welcome remarks for an admission event and utterly sardonic April Fools' columns for *The Georgia Guardian*, and then turn around and draft an annual report for the Board of Trustees that evinced a rare complexity of mind and an understanding of the vagaries of recruiting at the dawn of the twenty-first century. At executive leadership retreats, which can be plodding, dull affairs, it was Pam who convinced other vice presidents to dress in Village People costumes and perform a version of "Y.M.C.A." that she'd written new lyrics for, called, of course, "S.C.A.D."

She was a wonder, a gift.

On her office desk stood a plaque with a Churchill quote that read, "Never, never, never give up." This was the spirit of her leadership, when speaking to staff about a video or photo spread that still needed work. "We can do this," she'd say, rolling up her sleeves, ordering pizza, getting to work when someone else in her role would've left the staff members to solve the problem themselves.

"You're a great boss," I told her.

"I just feel like they're my friends," she said. "I want all of them to soar."

She always had the perfect turn of phrase, the perfect words.

Until the day she had no words.

"What is it?" I said.

Something was wrong.

"What?"

The year was 2003. We'd been through so much. We'd weathered those difficult times and watched as the sun rose on new days, as our careers changed, our families grew. Even the dark moments gave birth to new lights. Pam married again after she moved to Savannah, then divorced, another difficult moment, and yet out of that marriage came her third child, a beautiful boy, Adam, who inherited her love of invention and gift for song. These moments brought joy, and soon the university had entered what would be the single greatest period of growth in SCAD history, welcoming more than ten thousand students. We were flying high.

"I'm sick," she said, one day, sitting in my office at Lai Wa Hall.

"What?"

Pam, she of boundless energy, was never sick.

"Ovarian cancer," she said.

She took my hand, and we sat there, sun shining through the windows, a day so beautiful you thought your heart might break, and we listened to the sounds of leaves and wind and spring. I knew if I held her hand and didn't let go, then we could maybe stay like that forever, there, together.

I closed my eyes, and made a wish.

The first night she came home from the hospital—when I was

still a preschooler—I vowed to protect her from nightmares and under-the-bed monsters and heated burners and thorny bushes. After all, I was her big sister. I could protect her from anything.

...

I wanted to know all test results, medications, doctors' instructions, nurses' tips, and aspects of treatment to research further. On planes, in beds, waiting in traffic, I drained battery after battery of every device that could provide information, and I made notes, on hotel notepads, napkins, church bulletins, while the Reverend Jim Giddens prayed for our family.

Her doctor, Don Gallup, was wise and gifted, alchemizing life through the combination of treatments, medications, and nutrition that worked best for Pam's changing condition—a good day, a good week, a bad day, a better day, a great month, a terrible month. Our family has always been private, and it simply wasn't in our DNA to go around sharing every intimate detail of illness, treatment, suffering.

"We need your prayers," my mother and I would tell those who asked, and leave it at that. For Pam, hearing other people's stories was what brought her back to life from each torturous treatment. She had no need to recount every pain, the hours of unimaginable agony.

She and I slipped out of the office together for her first chemo treatment, not wanting to make a fuss, not wanting to worry the staff. We sat there, alone, not talking, and as soon as the IV began to drip, she passed out.

"Pam?" I said, panicking. Was this it? The end?

But a few minutes later, she was up and out of the treatment center, weak but smiling, and back at work. "Work makes me happy," she said, weakly, but with a comforting, playful lilt in her voice that no disease could suppress.

"You scared me," I said.

"That's my job, keeping you on your toes."

She got worse, then better, much better.

We blinked, and a year passed, then two, then three. She was healthy, the sun was shining. She even remarried again.

The university's thirtieth anniversary came and went, and our mother's ninetieth birthday in the very same year. Pam was now the senior vice president for marketing and enrollment management. In just over twenty years at the university, she had gone from a staff of one to leading a staff of nearly one hundred, deploying legions of recruiters everywhere from Anchorage to Argentina, Toulouse to Taiwan. I worried that it was too much for her, but she said no. She wanted to keep working. And then, while presiding over a presentation at Trustees Theater in the spring of 2010, Pam passed out on stage.

She was sick again, the doctors said. She pressed on, and we remained arm in arm, but I found myself fearfully worrying. Few people knew it was as bad as it was. Many staff had no idea that during a phone conference, she'd be participating from the car, on the way to chemo, or from her home office, where she could be more comfortable, where I would come sit with her when she was alone, to entice her to eat a bit. Our little house on the prairie had grown quiet, sorrowful, and we told stories that made us happy again, her weak laughter still bright enough to fill a room with light. The stories we told were not imaginary, not in castles or teepees or mud huts, not anymore. No, these stories were true stories, taking place in childhood bedrooms, on Mississippi front porches, on university stages, with an auditorium full of families and faculty and students in regalia. This was not make-believe. This was our life.

In May 2010, she stood at her beautiful daughter's wedding. On October 1, 2011, she died.

Her funeral took place on a Tuesday at the Skidaway Island United Methodist Church. So many members of the SCAD family were shocked.

"The last time I saw her, all she talked about were her children," they said.

"She wanted to know how I was feeling, since my surgery," they said.

"She asked about my plans after graduation."

I'd never seen that many people in one sanctuary—staff, faculty, alumni she'd recruited, who'd come to SCAD because of her, a vast and happy army of love filling the church. While eulogies filled the air, all I could do was close my eyes and wish myself back to that little house in Atlanta, when we brought my new sister home, when I'd looked in that little baby's eyes and saw myself, my soul, my twin.

"She's too delicate for you to hold," Mom had said.

"I won't break her," I said, crying, and remembering, I cried.

In the last days of Pam's life, once more she was tiny, fragile there on her white pillow, my beautiful sister, suddenly so small, her body the size of a girl's again. I saw her beloved children, Kevin, Kimberly, and Adam, help her stand up, walk with her to the porch to enjoy the air, and that's when I knew. She was not the breakable one. It was we who were fragile. It was she who remained strong.

Near the end, we kept saying "I love you" to one another, when she awoke in the morning, following afternoon naps, before she fell asleep in the evenings.

"You will have to be the one to say it last," she said.

I watched as she moved away from me, beginning another journey, her spirit lifting from the bed, departing the same way she'd come, suddenly, back into the blue.

In my office, I keep her Bible, her name engraved in gold foil on the front, Pam's little notes tucked inside. I've kept her voice mails on my cellphone, and I listen to them from time to time, so I can keep the memory of her beautiful voice with me forever, a voice full of song. When I dream, I dream of strange new melodies we haven't played yet, songs that live only in the heart. I think of those warm summer nights, her dancing on a porch while I played, and sometimes I wake, late at night, to the echo of soft bare feet on a slat floor, the plink of a piano in my ears, and I think I hear her, see her, smell her hair.

I know I'll see her one day.

I know we'll play together again.

Until then, I'll be waiting, with bitten lip and squinted eyes, looking up, skyward, waiting once more to see my sister.

Chapter Sixteen

The Bee and the Acorn

These days, I find answers mostly in metaphors, images secreting away seeds of truth, acorns scattered about the soft ground of spring.

"Mighty oaks from little acorns do grow," as they say.

The whole city of Savannah, where it all began for us, is a riotous garden of centurion live oaks, trees so strong and wide that they take on the aspect of benevolent titans, standing in the squares, along our lanes, shouldering the burden of the Southern sun. We photograph them, touch them, marvel at the city they make possible. Their age is measured in epochs, years we cannot comprehend. When did they stop being acorns, tiny forgettable things, and become timeless?

Many years ago, when I commissioned Steven Myers to draw a crest for the university, I asked him to include a bee and an acorn in the design. The bee, our mascot, defies logic—a fat little creature that isn't supposed to fly, yet does. Bees are busy. They build, collaborate, are drawn to beauty and color, and bounce across the summer. And what bees make is sweet, full of light.

Next to the bee is the acorn, laughably insignificant at first, one of thousands of hopeful ideas in a world full of them, most of them trampled. But then maybe in thirty or forty years, you look up and there it is, an oak, still young, but with strength that will carry it across the centuries. This university is nearing its fortieth year, and we are no longer the acorn—that fragile seedling, with only the potential for greatness, strength, sheltering boughs, nests for fledgling professionals. We stand tall. SCAD is young still, but with a vigor, resilience, and beauty that has surprised us all. I've learned the hard way not to make predictions.

"This building is way too big," I said of the Armory, now Poetter Hall, and I was wrong. Then and there, I decided to stop making predictions. Instead, I would focus on the present. I recently read a piece in the *New Yorker*, the text of a speech delivered to young writers, in which the speaker quotes the only useful advice he ever received:

"Have a vision, and cleave to it."

If I've done anything right in my life, it's been clinging to the mission and vision of this university, my belief that every aspect of SCAD could be useful and beautiful, equal parts delight and design. Meaningful and purposeful. While other universities have missions that are broad or vague, not so at SCAD. Ours is simple and clear as a bell:

> *SCAD exists to prepare talented students for professional careers, emphasizing individual attention in a positively oriented university environment.*

By holding fast to that clear and simple mission, miracles have happened that none of us could ever have predicted. I always believed SCAD would be great, yes, absolutely, ours would be the finest arts university in the world. But still, to see it every day with my own eyes, the people and places of SCAD in all their brilliance, takes my breath away.

I could not have predicted our size, that we would now have twelve thousand students in North America and Europe and Asia, or that we'd have students studying online, from the decks of battleships, in the outback of Oz, from the top of Taipei 101. I couldn't have predicted we'd have classrooms in ancient caves, or the way technology would change art education, with degree programs we never could have fathomed in 1978, like motion media design, service design, and themed entertainment design.

I surely couldn't have predicted that SCAD would find a home in Hong Kong, in an august structure that once housed a courthouse and jail cells, and that this new SCAD location would become so deeply integrated into the creative and professional community of Asia's World City.

I most definitely could not have predicted we would reinvent the admission process by creating videos and virtual reality headsets for all prospective students to experience every SCAD location in 360 degrees from their own homes and bedrooms, using a smartphone's internal sensors to create a unique perspective for each user.

You can't predict that stuff.

Maybe Isaac Asimov could have, maybe Arthur C. Clarke, but not me. I definitely couldn't have predicted we would have athletics at this university, much less national championships.

National championships in swimming, equestrian, lacrosse, and more. At an art school.

Yeah, right.

I couldn't have predicted that early collaborations and real-world work like our historic preservation initiative with the First African Baptist Church on Sapelo Island would lead to the university-wide embrace of collaboration among, for example, the departments of industrial design and sequential art, which would lead to the development of the SCAD Collaborative Learning Center and sponsored projects bringing students and faculty together with clients as diverse as Chick-fil-A, Hewlett-Packard, Microsoft, NASA, and the Centers for Disease Control and Prevention.

At an art school.

I couldn't have predicted all the magical moments of the Savannah Film Festival, such as Liam Neeson holding court on a Broughton Street sidewalk for a crowd of students who were transfixed because he really was as tall as he looked in the movies, or Ian McKellen appearing on stage for a roomful of young people who could not breathe for anticipation of what would come next.

And he stood up.

And they waited.

And he said it.

"YOU SHALL NOT PAAAAASS!"

And the crowd went wild.

Nor could I have predicted I'd sit in on a master class with Mike Myers and watch him play improvisation games with our giddy students, pretending to ride invisible horses across unseen prairies while the rest of us fell out of our chairs laughing.

And I most surely couldn't have predicted I'd conduct class observations with André 3000. "What do I call him?" I asked my staff. "Mr. 3000? Mr. Benjamin?"

"You should call him Ice Cold," one staff member, J.J. Waller, said, only half joking.

When I think of all the visitors who have shared their wisdom with our students—Sidney Poitier, Edward Albee, Peter O'Toole, Whoopi Goldberg, Alec Baldwin, Tom Wolfe, Nora Ephron, Robert Redford, Glenn Close—I am, more than anything, humbled.

I know this: I couldn't have predicted the twists and turns of my own life, the rending of what seemed eternal, the loss of my little sister, and the loss of my dear mother only three months later.

My mother, Willie May Lewis Poetter, was ninety-three years old. Surrounded by family, she died at home; her last days were spent looking out the window toward fig trees planted by my father.

In those last weeks before they died—only months apart—the half days had become whole, from the office to Pam's house, to sit with my sister, to make her comfortable, then to my mother's house, to read to her, look at her bills, handle what I could, two vigils for the two women who'd helped me become myself, twin pillars, and now the pillars were gone, and the portico where I'd taken shelter threatened to collapse, and I felt terribly alone and would have wandered into a fog and never come back, had it not been for Glenn and my children and dear friends around me.

I'd always stood in the midst of mother and father and sister, all helping, working together. There was no line between work and home.

"We're just itinerant laborers," Mom would say in those early years. "We work half days."

"Half days?" people would say, setting up her punchline.

"Yes," she'd say. "We work twelve hours a day instead of twenty-four."

I'd miss that fire. I'd miss that love.

Of the SCAD founders, I was the last one here.

...

"We are your family," a faculty member wrote to me, in a letter.

I've thought a lot about that word: *family*.

The character and spirit of my family had built and shaped this university and changed the tide of higher education. In 1978, everything about us was unorthodox, strange, outsider, a focus on professional career preparation without sacrificing liberal learning.

We taught students how to stand and speak and present their work, how to shake hands and build relationships. At an art school.

An art school.

The nerve.

And now, decades later, it seemed that everything we'd been ridiculed and mocked for was now being cited as the reason for our success. Along the way, there'd been the occasional charge of nepotism, the claim that SCAD only hired and promoted family members, a charge more confusing than anything. What did anyone expect, that we would try to start something as risky and tenuous as a new college with—what? Strangers?

The reality of our family soon spilled over the edges of meaning and became a metaphor, for example, when students like Alaine Daniel brought her young daughter to my office. "What should I do?" she said, desperate, anxious. "The babysitter fell through."

"I'll watch her," I said.

"She has a Barbie," Alaine said. "And some crayons and stuff."

Somewhere else, it might've seemed ridiculous for the academic dean to babysit for a student, but not here. Besides, my own children were there, too, napping under desks, rolling paint across the walls. Sure, Marisa and John Paul sometimes asked why they had to help clean or move desks, and I told them.

"Because anything worth doing is worth doing well. Everyone can help."

Saturdays, we'd all get up early and go to the post office to collect SCAD mail. Marisa and John Paul would tear through piles of junk mail and bills in search of real mail, the best kind: letters from students, applications for admission to SCAD. They helped open them, stacking them by region, loved reading about what each student wanted to study, where each was from. The city names were exotic, alien.

Santa Barbara, California.

Las Cruces, New Mexico.

Ocean Springs, Mississippi.

Cartagena, Colombia.

Cape Town, South Africa.

And by the time my first two children had grown up, graduated, launched their own careers, Madison and Trace were just as involved as their older siblings were: Madison, in a hotel ballroom in Hong Kong, standing offstage with SCAD honorary professor Jackie Chan, transfixed by the lion dance in the front of the room, and Trace, quizzing Geoffrey Fletcher about the making of *Precious*. In all these moments, Glenn is the beaming father, his lapels as sharp as his smile.

Our work is our home, our home is our work, our work is our family.

My sister and mother and father are gone, our family transformed by time and loss and love. In those early days of mourning, I took comfort in stories, sitting with family, sharing memories. We talked about the early days, when time had no meaning and grief had no quarter, when children smelled of grass and sweat, and Sundays were filled with food and stories, stories of sitting with students who wept after romantic breakups, of inviting international students to our home for Thanksgiving.

And I remember burying dear friends, like professor Ben Morris.

In the days after the funeral, his partner, Don Mondanaro, was alone, grieving, lost.

"Tell us what you need," I said. "Let's get you out of the house. Let's go somewhere."

"I'd sort of like to go bowling," he said.

And we called up the captain of the university's faculty bowling team, architectural history professor Jeff Eley, and we went bowling, and I was bad enough at it that we managed to get Don to laugh a little, and pretty soon we were laughing so hard we forgot to keep score, which was probably for the better.

I don't know. Is SCAD a family? It sure feels like it to me.

...

"What do you do all day?" Marisa once asked me, when she was seven or eight.

"Oh, I work."

"Yeah, I know, but what do you *do* all day?"

Trace asked me that, too, not long ago, and I opened up the folder my assistant hands me at the end of every day, a simple blue file folder with my homework in it—my schedule for the following day, any letters I should review, agendas for the next day's meetings. This particular folder was thin, containing only my daily schedule, rather unremarkable.

9 A.M. .... Correspondence

11 A.M. .... Videoconference with SCAD Atlanta

11:30 A.M. .... Review Board of Trustees remarks

12:30 P.M. .... Lunch

1 P.M. .... Commencement rehearsal at Savannah Civic Center

2 P.M. .... Review Delta "On Creativity" interviewee list

2:30 P.M. .... Review itineraries for Atlanta and Lacoste

3 P.M. .... Class observations

5 P.M. .... Outstanding Graduates Luncheon walk-through

The problem with this schedule is that it doesn't begin to tell the story of what I did that day, or any day in my life here, all the interstitial moments, the flying from flower to flower, searching out the brightest spots across the university, the places in need of pollinating, encouraging each flower to open and share its gifts, its best self.

Let me tell you what I really did on that warm day in late May.

I rose at six, made breakfast for Madison and Trace and Glenn. Madison now has a mind for medicine, but she could do anything. On this morning, she was a teacher, helping Trace review his Latin while I padded around the kitchen cracking eggs.

Trace is enraptured by Cirque du Soleil. When I looked at him, turning the words of his Latin into a song there at the breakfast table, his eyes dreaming of imaginary audiences and costumes, I saw many future students of our university, sitting at breakfast tables the world over, starry-eyed and dreaming of making something beautiful.

Soon, Madison was walking to class, a block away, while Glenn drove Trace to school. I dressed for work and saw a text from John Paul. He rarely texted this early, and my heart dropped, but only for a moment, when I remembered: He was in Hong Kong. It was seven o'clock in the evening there. I looked at my phone and saw a photograph of a student model in front of a green screen, a monitor in the foreground. The text read:

"Good morning—check out our first fashion shoot @ SCAD HK!!!"

I got into my car to drive to work, throwing my purse and bag into the passenger seat, and out fell the remarks I was to deliver at commencement. I had made some changes the night before, but sometimes I change too much.

"That's why we love you," my staff says, with irony, when they catch me turning draft No. 19 into draft No. 20, or adding commas to invitations we receive in the mail, removing surplus apostrophes. I sometimes have the bad habit of editing emails—emails that other people have sent me. My pen is drawn to these documents, magnetically, spiritually, and I start editing, cutting excess words, rescuing modifiers that have been dangled off the edges of sentences.

"Are you editing junk mail again?" they ask, catching me in the act.

"My desire for excellence is boundless," I say.

Honestly, there's always room for improvement. In everything.

I arrived at the office and settled down for two hours of reading and writing correspondence, letters and emails that my staff have printed out. Typically, I write my replies in the margins, at the bottom, on the back, with a Pilot Varsity fountain pen, my favorite pen. The art of the personal letter is a dying one, and I need and love my time alone, in the morning, writing these notes, replies, cards, letters, some typed, some handwritten. I loathe form letters, the deadness of a letter written by a machine, its adverbs strewn haphazardly across the page, misspellings of the names of spouses, children, commas gone missing, or reproducing like rabbits.

On that morning, there were notes from recent guests to the university—guests who'd attended SCADstyle and the SCAD Fashion Show—as well as a card from parents sharing good news about their graduating son and his new job at Google. There were letters from alumni, telling me what they were doing, a photo of one wearing a SCAD T-shirt on the top of Kilimanjaro, another who'd sent a pair of men's mid-cut boots handmade by him in Brooklyn, with a note inviting me to visit his workshop. I admired the boots and drafted a response, inviting him to sell more products at shopSCAD in the United States or France.

"Or both!" I wrote.

I handed the stacks of letters to my assistant and stepped into the boardroom to videoconference with the vice president for SCAD Atlanta, Dr. Teresa Griffis, who came here nearly twenty-five years ago to teach English and who now leads our second North American location—with more than two thousand students, twenty-one academic departments, and fifty academic degree programs. She updated me on commencement plans for the weekend, and we discussed enrollment for the summer quarter. Commencement is always a busy day—we have a ceremony in Savannah at 9 a.m. and another in Atlanta at 6 p.m. and another in Hong Kong the following week.

"See you soon!" I said, waving to the screen.

Over lunch, I prepared for the board meeting on the following day, reviewing the presentation deck. I recited the remarks a few times, alone in my office. Nothing helps me edit like speaking the words aloud. Then I flipped open a book we'd created for an upcoming event and started editing. It was sixty pages long—a collection of photographs and quotes and captions and narrative—and it was in dire need of editing. A sample of my handwritten notes in the margins:

Seems too corporate, like an insurance company calendar. Make more joyful.

This is a beautiful design, but the font is too constricted.

Ask Glenn what he thinks of this layout.

Please mention here that Karl Lagerfeld donated all these works to SCAD.

I don't like the word strut. *What can we say instead? Dance? Parade?*

I sometimes wish I could go through every publication with its creators right there in the room with me. Verbal feedback is usually more effective, where our talented photographers and writers and editors and designers, many of them SCAD alumni, can hear the nuances of a comment, the spirit of a critique and not just the letter. But time is of the essence, and we are so large now that marginalia is how I provide much of my feedback these days, hoping the team understands what I'm saying, that I'm trying to encourage them, guide them.

I'd made it through five pages when my assistant pulled the book gently from my hands and explained I had a few last-minute meetings just added to my calendar.

"For when?"

"For now."

Meetings. Such a simple word, such an essential, central function of my work as president. Meetings with guests, visiting artists, candidates, board members, corporate partners, on and on the list goes—but my most important meetings are always, always with the faculty, staff, chairs, deans, vice presidents, students, and alumni from within the SCAD community. Half of my meetings are requested by others, so they can share a new idea to do something wild and brilliant, maybe, or get feedback on an early draft of a new initiative before they keep going down that road, while the other half of my meetings are requested by me.

Many of my most creative ideas are born in these meetings, asking the right question of the right person at the right time. In these conversations, I always advise that we pick up the idea under consideration, as though it were a three-dimensional object, turning and examining each facet and fact to discern possible advantages and anticipate possible difficulties. I try to look at every issue, every question, every challenge the way I look at a work of art—carefully, thoughtfully, playfully, joyfully, seriously.

On this particular day, a staff member requested a meeting to share terrific news: *CBS Sunday Morning* would soon be visiting SCAD for a segment on the university's historic role in the urban revitalization of Savannah.

"Wow!" I said. "Good, fabulous, amazing!"

Quickly, we discussed strategy. Whom should we suggest they interview? Faculty from architecture? Architectural history? Historic preservation? Which facilities should we make sure they see? What story do they want to tell? What story do we want to tell? We talked excitedly, shared ideas, reminisced about past TV and magazine interviews, the bloopers, the lessons learned, the sort of fantastically unscripted moments that happen at SCAD—no matter how much we prepare for guests! We laughed, made a to-do list, heard a knock. Our time was up. In a flash, thirty minutes had turned to sixty, and my assistant announced another last-minute meeting request, this one via videoconference.

I made my way back to the conference room and connected on the screen with my son, John Paul, who serves as vice president for strategy and innovation. He has incredible gifts for strategic thinking, for building relationships, and he's spent time working at every SCAD location. Today, he was on the other side of the world, helping staff at the Hong Kong location prepare for a few big end-of-quarter events.

"Greetings from Sham Shui Po!" he said.

It's still hard to believe we've had this thriving campus in Asia for more than five years now. It was getting close to midnight in Hong Kong, but you wouldn't have known it by looking at John Paul. And of course, I've received a few calls from Hong Kong at two or three in the morning, right in the middle of their workday. Sometimes they're up late, sometimes it's us. This is the reality of being a global institution.

"There's somebody coming your way I wanted you to know about," John Paul said, and he explained about a possible corporate partner—whom he'd met at the Mandarin Oriental a few weeks back, during a SCAD event at Art Basel Hong Kong—who was heading to the States and might be up for a meeting to discuss a future collaboration. "Somebody from his office will probably be reaching out for an appointment," he said. "Just wanted you to know."

"Thank you!" I said.

We chatted for a few minutes about my upcoming visit to Hong Kong for commencement, and then disconnected. His call made me think of all our locations. Not only the whole team in Hong Kong, but also Teresa in Atlanta, Cédric Maros in Lacoste.

"Call Cédric," I wrote in my notebook.

I'd recently promoted Cédric, a longtime staff member, to the role of director of SCAD Lacoste. I hadn't spoken with him in a couple of weeks, except by email. Things were clearly going well; we'd recently placed two of our American students in internships in Paris. But still, I wanted to hear from him how the students were doing in their final week of that life-changing quarter in the Luberon. It was evening already in Lacoste. I decided to wait. I'll call him later, I thought, when he's just walking up the stone streets to his office in the morning.

...

It's exhilarating to see what SCAD has in store for me every day, and to share my best ideas with the brilliant people around me, around the world, and it's exhausting.

In these conversations, I find myself using many allusions, idioms.

"Put all ten fingers in your gloves, not just one."

"This is not the Sistine Chapel. This is not *E.T.*"

"To make a pearl, sometimes we need a little irritant, a little grain of sand."

Also, I find myself drawing and diagramming to simplify and communicate complex ideas, like a philosophy professor at the chalkboard. In 2010, I reinvented our career and alumni services offices on the back of an envelope, showing with a timeline and flowchart how these two offices should in fact be one unified department, helping prepare students for jobs even before they enroll at SCAD. How the university could continue to work with them through very specific touchpoints and benchmarks through each year of their degree programs, through graduate school, and then five, ten, and fifteen years postgraduation. I communicated all this with an urgently rendered sketch, shared with key staff as quickly as it sprang forth from the workshop of my mind. I'm sure I still have this sketch somewhere.

In recent years, I've invited student, faculty, and alumni storyboard artists to be present for conferences and retreats to help us visualize and capture the ideas born in these important moments.

Yes, all this drawing and talking and asking and listening and laughing and wondering takes its toll. Early in my career, at the end of each day of teaching, I was "wore out" (as my grandmother Olive would have said) from simply joining ideas, bringing relevant knowledge tucked away in my head to the discussion, figuring out different ways to turn on the lightbulbs in my students' minds.

These days, I often feel the same way—just talked out, emptied of my best ideas, waiting to be filled up again. I come to work a filled-up vessel, with new ideas and ways of improving exploding out of my mind. By the end of the day, I am drained and my voice is a whisper.

But on that day, I still had my voice. For now.

We were late for the next event on my schedule, the graduation walk-through, and my assistant and I dashed to the Savannah Civic Center, joined by the graduates who would also be speaking. We practiced our speeches, tried our best to match the rhythm of the teleprompter. I gave them notes, asked them to give me notes. These students had been critiquing their classmates' work for four years, I reminded them; now it was time they critiqued the president's.

All around the arena, staff members were hanging banners, lights, readying the space for the graduates and their families, buzzing bees in the pale cornflower blue shirts of the SCAD physical resources team.

At our first commencement in 1981, we awarded a single Bachelor of Fine Arts degree in interior design to Juli Lee. At this commencement, we'd be awarding Bachelor of Arts, Bachelor of Fine Arts, Master of Arts, Master of Fine Arts, Master of Architecture, and Master of Urban Design degrees to more than two thousand graduates.

We slipped away to another meeting, this one with the creative direction team. A year ago, I'd started interviewing guests on camera—Arianna Huffington, Zac Posen, Xu Bing. We posted these short videos to YouTube, we met with Delta, and all of a sudden we're making in-flight videos for a major airline and its millions of passengers. But whom will we interview this time? The team shows me some names. I approve them all, add a few new ideas. Meeting adjourned.

I have to laugh. For so long, I was the stage manager of SCAD, behind the curtain, with the clipboard, writing and editing and urging in whispers, and while I am still doing much of the editing, somehow, reluctantly, I have also become the face of this place.

I could not have predicted that.

Next, my staff and I reviewed what would be happening in the coming weeks—business trips to our locations in Atlanta and Hong Kong to meet with students and staff and attend commencements, and then to Lacoste to encourage everybody there, participate in summer classes, and check in on physical resources improvements, which never stop, like me, because I was now back in the car with another staff member, Maggie, to visit classes.

"We're going to Photographic Bookmaking," Maggie said.

The students would be presenting a two-part final project of photography books, one handstitched, one professionally produced, she explained.

"The professor says it'd be great if you could participate in the critiques."

"Oh, good!"

In the hallway of Bergen Hall after our class visit, which took up most of the afternoon, I overheard students speaking in the classroom we'd just left.

"She *started* the school?" one asked. "That's crazy."

I'm sure the fact that I was here in the beginning, in the 1970s, makes me seem to our current students like I emerged from the Triassic. These students are younger than Taylor Swift. The year some of them were born, SCAD was already preparing for its twentieth anniversary. Have I been here that long? Will I stay here forever? I don't know. I'll always be involved somehow, I'm sure, but I can't do it forever, not at this pace. I know that.

Back in the car, I found time to edit a few more pages of the history of SCAD fashion, and soon we arrived at the Gryphon, where we'd have a lunch on Friday for the valedictorian, salutatorian, and other graduates and their families. The board would be joining us, and the events team wanted to get my thoughts on the new layout.

"Where will we stand to present the medals?" I asked.

They pulled out the podium and we rearranged tables, some of the server staff helping out. The staff members at Gryphon are students. We chatted. They were glad summer was almost here, in less than a week.

"Me too," I said.

"I need to sleep," one said.

"Me too."

I looked around at Gryphon, which we redesigned a few years before. We've operated this restaurant for decades now—first it was a bookstore and lunch counter, then a student coffee shop, then an upscale tea room for the university community and the public. When we started SCAD, this place had been a pharmacy. I remember huddling across the street in the Armory long, long ago during the hurricane, holding Marisa, watching the pharmacy through the uncanny dark of midday as bits of its façade ripped away and went sailing down Bull Street.

We stepped outside, and a breeze blew across my memory, and in an instant, I forgot what year it was. Had the years passed us this quickly?

I drove home, a few blocks away. Everywhere I looked, every window I passed, I saw myself in the reflections of glass, in the design of a building, in the hum of a river of students streaming out into the street after class. Arriving home, dizzy and weary from the day's work, I found dinner waiting on me. Glenn had cooked.

"What did you do today?" Trace asked.

"A lot," I said.

When dinner was over, I did the dishes alone. I love my dishwashing time, undistracted by a phone or a file folder or staff members with questions. And soon, the dishes were clean, the homework done, and it was dark outside, the long spring day over. Glenn found me in the parlor, finishing up my edits on an exhibition catalog.

"Good night," he said, kissing me on the forehead.

I was too wired to sleep and turned on my iPad. It was a good time to catch up on the day's emails, when the rest of the world had stopped looking at their screens. Much of managing the university happens here, in emails to staff members, providing direction.

I wrote to enrollment staff about our record-setting week for admission deposits ("Six hundred deposits? Wow. What can we do to tell the SCAD story to more students?") and wrote another email to a retiring faculty member ("I hope you can stay involved here.") and another to a new faculty member, in response to a thank-you card expressing his eagerness to get into the classroom this fall ("Your future students share your enthusiasm, I know!") and one email in reply to a graduating senior from Iran whose life had been changed profoundly by coming to SCAD ("Your story's a powerful reminder what a gift education is—to all of us, everywhere, from every nation.") and one to museum staff about an upcoming exhibition ("Think about it: Most people out in the universe of public consciousness assume a museum in Savannah would be stodgy. We have to show them the SCAD museum is anything but.").

Leading a university is fundamentally no different from leading a classroom—you stand in front of everyone and explain what's to be done and why. The why is key. That's the big vision stuff. But you don't merely stay up there in front of everybody, casting visions; you move around the room, seeking out those who need more direction, kneeling down with those doing the work, at eye level, hearing their concerns, walking them through the steps, through each problem, if they need it. In my communication with faculty and staff, I work ceaselessly to put their daily work into context, the bigger picture, the larger story of SCAD. Here's an excerpt of an email I sent that night, to two university leaders:

*Been thinking a lot about fashion photo, fashion styling,
fashion film. I'm seeing an active need for photographers
to know how to style. Had an interesting conversation
with a photography graduate student the other day.
Very impressive.*

*We need to ensure students stay current with digital
processes and contemporary movement in the industry.
Ergo, styling. Please research all the most in-demand film
and photo needs—for students postgraduation—and
ensure we're preparing students for those opportunities.*

The question of fashion photography and styling had been
buzzing around my mind for a while, waiting to alight somewhere,
and this conversation with a student, plus previous conversations
with alumni, gave these ideas a place to land. Sharing these ideas
and directives with my team—explaining not only what I want
them to do next, but why—keeps everyone flying forward, in the
same direction, our faces pointed toward what's next for SCAD.

I sent the email and rubbed my eyes. I was done, for now.

I crept up to the bedroom where Glenn was fast asleep. I felt
like the luckiest woman alive, filled with joy. It was time to sleep.
This little bee was tired.

Commencement was in a few days.

The beginning of something, the ending of something.

I closed my eyes and tried to remember Maya Angelou standing at the podium a few years ago, the vast room as still as a church.
We all waited for her to speak, but instead she sang "When the
Saints Go Marching In."

"You all look like angels this morning," she said to the students.

There in the dark, my heart leapt just thinking of that moment.

...

Two days later, John Lasseter made our hearts leap again, when he told a story about one of his most famous creations. He held for all to see a tattered and much-loved Woody doll from *Toy Story*—missing a boot and his hat, but still standing tall. John, whose son was graduating from SCAD that day, reminded us that as artists, designers, and educators, our work—like Woody's—has heart.

"SCAD has given you a great gift: the time and opportunity to develop in yourself new ways of seeing and thinking," he said. "You have the capacity and obligation to make the most of that gift—and your own unique gifts. Congratulations. Go out and change the world."

We stood. We cheered. For John, for SCAD, for each other. And then, silence, and a booming, pulsing heartbeat, and a brilliant, gemlike projection on the giant screens, high overhead.

The lights flashed, and the SCAD Drumline materialized on stage and started to play a jazzy, driving beat, while acrobats descended from the ceiling and the confetti cannons popped, the arena erupting in jubilant celebration, student performers twirling through the aisles, enormous glowing beach balls bouncing across the sea of smiling faces, and I looked out into the arena to see thousands of graduates and their families, our family, the global SCAD family, standing, swaying, singing, clapping, wiping away tears of joy.

In these moments, I try to remind myself how lucky I am, all the memories and moments I never could have predicted, the life I never thought I could have, and what I find myself remembering most are the small moments, the dance of light over a square of sidewalk chalk, the squeeze of my mother's hand while walking in her final commencement, the sweet smell of my sister's room. My memory is a forest of oaks, and I wander through, touching each moment with fondness and gratitude to have lived here, walked here.

"We did it!" one graduate said to another, off to my right, as our joyful processional bounced down the aisle through the jubilation, down through a whole swirling sea of regalia.

"Can you believe it?" another student said, to my left, dancing, reaching up to touch the falling confetti.

"I love you guys!" said another, embracing no fewer than three classmates around her.

I reached out my arms and high-fived everyone down the aisle, smiling, laughing, the tears already streaming, my heart bursting.

I am grateful for a family that lifts me up, loves me unconditionally, for children who hug me for no good reason, for a husband who holds my hand, for a sister who made me a better woman, for a mother and father who poured their very souls into my dream and made it a reality.

I am grateful for friends who can help me cut through the noise of the spinning world to hear those voices of love and joy that have something to say, friends who have brought beauty into my life at every turn, through their stories, their smiles.

I am grateful for those schoolchildren so many years ago who taught me how to be a teacher, whose genuine marveling at the world woke up my own sense of wonder, driving me to want something new, paving the way for this university, this jewel, this SCAD.

I am grateful for the blessing and gift of imagination, that boundless spirit running through space and time that drives us all to make, dream, build, tell, and I am grateful that this is what my colleagues and I get to do every day, to help students make, dream, build, tell.

I am grateful to all those who helped me create SCAD, those who corrected me as a child or inspired me to do more. They may not know how much they have impacted SCAD and its thousands of bright minds, merry hearts, and growth of good in the world.

Yes, there's always room for improvement. I am grateful for the difficulty, the hurt, the challenges throughout my life.

Mostly I am grateful for my colleagues, the faculty and staff and board members and volunteers who have knowledge and experience far surpassing my own and who have been deeply generous in sharing their gifts with me, devoting themselves to helping create truly enchanted learning experiences and environments for SCAD students.

Our marching line reached the rear of the arena, making its way back to the greenroom, and I did something I wasn't supposed to do. I stopped.

I stopped, and turned around, and looked.

"Keep going!" someone behind me said.

But I wanted to see.

Glowing white beach balls bounced around the room, and confetti danced down through the air, and the screens exploded with light and color. It was heavenly, all the joy in one place, all of it for SCAD. There, amid the host of exultation, I felt my mother and father and sister standing there with us, beaming, cheering, hearts lifted high, eyes shining.

One more academic year over.

And I can't wait to do it again.

Acknowledgments

My life's work—the building and shaping of the finest arts university in the world—is a collaboration of the highest order. I stand in the midst of a great host of partners and colleagues and champions who have cheered me on, encouraged and counseled and taught me, eased my hurting, lifted my heart, pointed me toward the horizon, helping SCAD continue to make history, buck tradition, and reinvent higher education.

I must first thank my mother and father and sister, who never doubted that I could do great things, even when I doubted myself, and who raised me up, constantly and unfailingly, throughout my life. And I thank my family—Glenn, Marisa, Brandon, John Paul, Madison, Trace, Kimberly, Michael, Kevin, Adam—who lift me still. I love you.

I also want to thank the friends who have loved my family and held our hands through the years: Charles and Dottie Redmond, Lessie Bryce, Nancy Verell, Martha Enzmann, Karen Butch, and all the teachers who taught me the necessity of imagination and grit, especially Peggy Mayfield and Connie Bradley. And I must thank two people who helped SCAD find its first home in the Armory, Jackie Horne and Henry Kennedy.

Thank you to past and present board members, friends of the university, volunteers, and community partners, whose hearts for service are humbling and everlasting. Your hearts have made SCAD possible: Doris Beck, Veronica Biggins, Michael Bishop, Paul Bradley, Garry Brown, John Burger, Bernie Casey, Chan Lai Wa, Tom Crites, Domenico and Eleanore De Sole, Frank Dickey, Dick and Judy Eckburg, Walter and Linda Evans, Alice Fisher, Pattie Graham, Nancy Herstand, Alison Hopton, Bob and Alice Jepson, P.J. Johnson, Fran Jones, Virginia Kiah, W.W. Law, Edd Miller, Don Mondanaro, Bob and Sue Nardelli, Charlie and Marie Pepe, Bruce Phillips, John Proffitt, Sally Waranch Rajcic, Richard Rowan, Hildi Santo Tomás, Stuart Saunders, Steve Scheer, André Leon Talley, Tan and Özlem Tascioglu, Ann Tenenbaum, Arnold and

Lorlee Tenenbaum, Anita Thomas, Tom and Jeanne Townsend, Bill Trussell, Diane von Furstenberg, Bertie Wallace, Ronald Waranch, Jack Watson, Belle Wheelan, Albie Whitaker, and many others.

I bow with humble adoration to the SCAD family, those students, alumni, faculty, and staff who live this dream with me every day. When I think of you, I hear the words of my father's most beloved poem, Tennyson's "The Charge of the Light Brigade."

> *When can their glory fade?*
> *O the wild charge they made!*
>   *All the world wondered.*
> *Honour the charge they made.*

Together, we renew this charge every day, in the classrooms and galleries and studios of SCAD and around the world. You are noble and truly a wonder and a blessing, each of you: Barbara Allen, Judith Ott Allen, Phil Alletto, Margo Ames, Robert Belloir, Margy Betz, Betsey Brairton, Maureen Burke, David Busch, Chuck Chewning, Pete Christman, Madeline Collins, Beth Concepción, Jeff Eley, Victor Ermoli, Roz Evans, Jim Falk, Tom Fischer, Hannah Flower, Catherine Fruisen, Andy Fulp, Hugh Gale, Maureen Garvin, Bobbie Gautreau, James Graham, Brad Grant, Tim Green, Raymond Greene, Lesley Hanak, Traci Haymans, Trevor Jenkins, Fran Jones, Laura Kennedy, Marcus Kenney, Margaret Kross, Juli Lee, Van Jones Martin, Lesa Mason, Frances McCommon, Steve Mineo, Deb and Steve Mosch, Julie Mueller-Brown, Erin O'Leary, Gokhan Ozaysin, Anthony Pace, David Pugh, Mark Rand, Becky Rowe, Katherine Sandoz, Carmen Stowers, Lew Tate, Judith Van Baron, J.J. Waller, Crystal Weaver, Pamela Wiley, Frances Wong, Josh Yu, and hundreds more men and women who have dedicated their lives to teaching, learning, and making the world a more beautiful, more inviting place. You are SCAD.

Thank you to the creative shamans who helped bring this book into the world: Emily Isabella, Harrison Scott Key, Hayley Harris, Jonathan Ashley Osborne, and Rosa Triolo. Thank you for using your wondrous talents to help me tell this story.

About the Author

Paula Wallace is the president and founder of the Savannah College of Art and Design, a private, nonprofit, accredited university for creative careers. Established in 1978, SCAD is the most comprehensive art and design university in the United States, with locations in Savannah and Atlanta, Georgia; Lacoste, France; and Hong Kong; as well as an award-winning eLearning program.

She served as academic dean and provost of SCAD for twenty-two years and has served as president of the university since 2000. As president, Wallace has led the university in unprecedented growth, more than doubling enrollment from fewer than five thousand students to more than twelve thousand students. Wallace created and championed many of the university's most popular annual events, including the Savannah Film Festival, SCAD deFINE ART, SCADstyle, the Sidewalk Arts Festival, and SCAD aTVfest.

As the university grows, Wallace continues to advance the SCAD legacy of historic preservation, which has been recognized with prestigious awards from the National Trust for Historic Preservation, the International Coalition of Art Deco Societies, the American Society of Interior Designers, UNESCO, and the American Institute of Architects. The university's interior design programs are highly ranked, with the SCAD undergraduate interior design program earning *DesignIntelligence's* top ranking for five consecutive years.

Wallace has authored several children's books and two interior design titles—*Perfect Porches* and *A House in the South*. Among many awards and honors, she has been named among the world's "30 Most Admired Educators" by *DesignIntelligence* and "Entrepreneur of the Year" by Ernst & Young, and was awarded the inaugural Elle Decor Vision Award. Wallace has been appointed a Chevalier dans l'Ordre des Palmes Académiques by the French Embassy in the United States of America, and the Georgia Historical Society named her a 2015 Georgia Trustee. She currently serves on the National Advisory Board of the National Museum of Women in the Arts in Washington, D.C.

Wallace earned a Bachelor of Arts degree from Furman University and Master of Education and Education Specialist degrees from Georgia State University; she also was awarded an honorary Doctor of Laws from Gonzaga University. Wallace's husband is Glenn, and her four children are Marisa, John Paul, Madison, and Trace.

Follow Wallace on Twitter and Instagram at @paulaswallace. To learn more about SCAD, visit scad.edu.

The Savannah College of Art and Design is a private, nonprofit, accredited university offering more than one hundred academic degree programs in forty-two majors at locations in Atlanta and Savannah, Georgia; Hong Kong; Lacoste, France; and online via SCAD eLearning.

SCAD enrolls more than twelve thousand undergraduate and graduate students from more than one hundred countries. SCAD's innovative curriculum is enhanced by advanced, professional-level technology, equipment, and learning resources, as well as opportunities for internships, professional certifications, and collaborative projects with corporate partners. In 2015, the prestigious Red Dot Design Rankings placed SCAD in the top five universities in the Americas and Europe. Career preparation is woven into every fiber of the university, resulting in a superior alumni placement rate. In a survey of Spring 2014 SCAD graduates, 97 percent of respondents reported being employed, pursuing further education, or both within ten months of graduation.